Ragged Triptych

poems by Marc Pietrzykowski

Ragged Triptych

Copyright © 2015 by Marc Pietrzykowski

Cover design: Marc Pietrzykowski

All rights reserved. No part of this book may be reproduced in any form by any electronic or mechanical means including photocopying, recording, or information storage and retrieval without permission in writing from the author.

ISBN-13: 978-0692487020
ISBN-10: 0692487026

visit the author virtually:
www.marcpski.com

Printed in U.S.A

for Ashley

Other books by Marc Pietrzykowski

...and the whole time I was quite happy (poetry)

The Logic of Clouds (poetry)

Following Ghosts Upriver (poetry)

Music Box Dancer (fiction)

Conflagrations (poetry, with Mary Leary)

No Tribe, No Tribute (poetry)

The Emissary (fiction)

Straddling the Sibyl (poetry)

Kindness is Never Small (poetry)

visit the author virtually at www.marcpski.com

My first three books of poetry, the titles of which are listed at the left, I published with three different presses. I decided to compile them here into a single volume because I was curious to see how they read as chapters, rather than as individual books, and because I wanted to make a more inexpensive version available to readers who were interested in any of those three books. Like many poets, I am somewhat obsessive about my development as an artist, and like many poets, I labor under the impression that readers still exist that also find value in considering the same kinds of aesthetic questions. And, like most poets, I am suspect I am deluding myself, but self-delusion is the least of my worries. Enjoy!

Marc Pietrzykowski
6/6/2015

Contents

....and the whole time I was quite happy

part 1

A Good Toss	15
The Start of a Refrain	16
The Utilitarian	18
The Source Of Many A Fire	19
When Loverman Pulls Up	22
And We Moved Like Heat	23
A Glimpse of The Future	25
Three That Moved Me	26
Feeling More Than One	28
Among the Ten Thousand May Be One That Returns Us	29
13	31
And It Never Stopped Snowing	33

part 2

The First Lesson	35
Get On With It	38
LSD Madrigal	40
Staples	42
My Hometown Is Filled With Crazy People	43
Maukin at the Harvest Home	46

part 3

How About A Little Fire?	49
Goodbye, Gentleman Farmers	51
Dog, Cat, Man, Bird, Bear, Wind, Day	53
Lost In The Land of the Holy Ones	55
Learning to Sleep Through It	62
Hiding	64
A Dead Giveaway	66
Life On The Cube Farm	68
The Insult	70
The Procession	71

The Logic of Clouds

Stratus

Neither Here Nor There 75
The Anachronist 76
Revolutionary Intent and the Appetite of the Modern We..... 77
The Benefit of Yelling Off the Porch at Passers-by 78
Doing the Books for the Galactic Sideshow. 79
Bucky, Near Infirm From Years Underground, ... 81
Resurfaces to Visit the Deathbed of Captain America 81
The Nervous Bride Talks To Her Guardian Angel 83
The Perpetual Attrition of the 19th Regiment 84
The Janitor Takes His Rest 85
The Imposition of Appetite 87
The Triumph of Magical Thinking 88
Regarding The Breach 89
A Blister Forms.. 92
USA: Two Views, 2003 94
Death And the Soccermom 95
The Mower Obeys The Covenant. 99
The Noggin.. 100

Nimbus

In Praise of the Plague, That It Might Be Pleased and Spare
Me, and My Family 105
The Tyranny of Species 106
The Tyranny of Loved Ones 107
The Tyranny of the Firmament 109
Variations on the Theme of World Domination 110
Making Much of Time 111
The Pinup Girl, Later.................................... 112
A Conceit For Middle-Managers 114
The Last Request.. 115
In Praise of Breast Implants 116
In Praise of the Hummer.. 117
In Praise of the 128 oz. Porterhouse Steak. 119

Christmas Market Afternoon. 120
And That, My Friends, Is The Afterlife. 121
On Donating A Kidney. 122
The Party Begins 123
Young Mothers Aboard the Train 125
To Lie and Wait. 127
On the Fermentation Of Grains And Other Things 129
At the Lake In Wintertime. 131
Lunatics Held In Isolation 132
Hallucinate Their Own Omnipotence.. 132
In the Train Station Watching Footage of a Plane
Striking a Building. 133
The cat has gone missing.. 135
Revisiting a Theme. 136
Waltzing Toward Slumber 137
Shepherd at Pause in the Rain-Shadow. 138

Following Ghosts Upriver

part 1

Following Ghosts Upriver, 1.. 141
Desire Algebraic 142
Good Friday. 144
Animal Logic and the Hub. 148
How I Almost Nodded Off (or, I imagine a baby rat
in my mouth as I wait for my beloved to come home).. 149
Executive Privilege.. 153
Research and Development 155
Mirabilia 156

part 2

Following Ghosts Upriver, 2.. 157
There's Never a Line. 160
At The Niagara County Landfill and Recycling Center
(or, The Believer Among Us). 162
Economic Development Seminar. .163

The Grinding Wears the Stone Down, Too 164
Ice Sculpture 166
In Praise of Winter. 167

part 3

Stare Decesis 169
Carnivalesque. 170
The Flare. 171
Strategy and Tactics 173
Lunar Spring Thaw 175
House and Door and Window .177
Sonnets Are Stupid. 178
Thank You For Showing Me The Way Home 179
The Frequency is in the Upper Reaches of the Band. 180
Following Ghosts Upriver, part 3 181
Little City Breakdown. 183

....and the whole time I was quite happy

originally published in 2007 by Zeitgeist Press

part 1

A Good Toss

Uncle Patrick thought it'd be funny to get the baby drunk,
but Uncle John was too drunk to do any laughing.
Aunt Cathy, the babysitter, was in the backyard with a mescaline grin.

Cathy's boyfriend Frank cried cause he pissed on a tree and heard it scream,
so he covered the trunk with shaving cream.
Uncle Patrick poured schnapps into the baby's throat—
the baby smiled and then pissed and shit all over the bed.

Uncle John was snoring. He was in the La-Z-Boy
when Grandpa came home and found the house nearly empty,
the booze all gone, Uncle John asleep, the backyard littered with bottles
and shaving cream, and the baby lying naked
on Grandpa's bed, lolling in a puddle of urine and feces.

Grandpa always made his bed like he'd done in the army.
Grandpa always made it bounce-a-nickle taut and no one dared touch it.
Grandpa grabbed the baby by the neck and threw it in the closet.

Uncle John woke up and heard the baby crying, then heard it stop
Annie came home from the movie and asked where her baby was.
"I don't know where everybody went," John said.

The Start of a Refrain

She's laid his clothes out on the bed—the pants
and shirt embroidered with smiling bears,
the socks pointing down to little boots
ready for bronzing—she's put them in order
and now leans against the mattress, touching
her swollen, puckering navel with a finger,
trying to imagine how he'll smell, wondering
if she'll be like her own mother, if they'll let her
keep him this time. *I'd like to see'em try
and take him away*, she whispers, and begins
to stuff the shirt and pants with balls of cotton.
A truck door slams and she jumps, crouches,
listens to her mother's voice: *That little
slut. Ain't having no bastard in this house.*
Right. Like Daddy'd never caught *her*, legs up
and wriggling beneath Mr. Kedalis
from next door, as though *she* never sobbed
the whole vodka-smeared Saturday night away
while her sister banged against the headboard
under Daddy's girth, three houses down.
Their voices stained the wallpaper, and she knew
she had to get away, only away, anywhere.

Slinking back to bed, she crawls beneath
the grey threadbare sheets and squeezes tight,
but not too tight, on the soft cotton-filled shirt
appliqued with happy bears standing in a circle.
Three days from now, on her eighteenth birthday,
she'll watch as the highway rips by beneath her,
drag deep on a Pall Mall, and wonder if
perhaps she should've stayed, seeing as how
the pimply boy beside her driving
his daddy's car will surely drop her off

at the bus station, then flee. *Don't need him
either,* needs no one but her own little man,
her own loved thing to hold and fuss over,
let them try and take him this time—when at last
they come to the door with their hands bent like hooks,
she knows exactly what she will say:
*don't you dare touch him, or I swear,
people everywhere will start hearing about
all those things you made me promise
never to tell a soul—*

The Utilitarian

By the time I was four, I could pour spaghettios
into a pan and cook'em up, but my hands were too small
to use our old can opener. I'd ask the Indian woman

who lived across the hall to do it, always answering her
that "my mother is at the movies right now,"
which she was, in a manner of speaking, transfixed

by the shadows moving across the floor, the words
someone else was mumbling in her skull, someone
who told her to take off her clothes and go hide

under the couch cushions stacked in a corner
and make animal noises. When she didn't feel so bad
she taught me to read, so by the time that I was five

I had the sneer of the gourmet and the blackened fingers
of the bibliophile. I've been eating and reading ever since.
It pays to learn how to keep the voices out by burrowing

into the silence of a book or meal, or else you might wind up
in a million pieces, wondering if the noise of some half-wit
crying in the distance is actually coming out of you.

The Source Of Many A Fire

There were two playgrounds within walking distance
    of the apartment that the welfare people found
for mother and myself. One, which could be seen from
    our window, was filled with screaming kids
and mothers who drank cans of beer and did each other's hair
    at the picnic table. Even in the summer
we had to wear shoes at that one cause of the glass
    and needles and dirty diapers spilling out
of the garbage cans. The other playground was clean and shone
    like water, or at least it seemed that way
from the road. We couldn't go there because mother
    was afraid to cross the pedestrian bridge
spanning the interstate, and the only other way to get there
    was to take three buses in a great loop around the city.
on my birthday mother gave me a plastic toy boat wrapped
    in the funny pages, and the man who would later
be my stepfather gave me a coloring book with pictures
    of dinosaurs, but no crayons. Then we went over
to his Dad's house, and they went inside and left me out in the car
    for so long I shit my pants on his naugahyde seats.
still, he was quite gentle about the whole thing since
    he wanted my mother, and to make it up
to us he bought popsicles and took mother and me
    to the special playground. I knew something was wrong
as soon as I walked through the gate—all the children seemed
    wise, somehow, worried about the state of their clothes,
playing intently in weird routines—and to be sure, not one of them
    wanted a damn thing to do
with a worn-out courderoy-wearing, homemade-haircut-having,
    smells-like-shit-and-Woolite burr-head like me.
that was the first time I heard the word 'trash' used
    in that birth-right tone of voice; a little girl with pigtails
even called me nigger, though I was whiter than she'd ever
    want to be. Mother loved being with the pinched
and proper ladies who sat discussing future scholarships

and weekends at the cottage; she never noticed,
the way her boyfriend and I did, that she was absolutely excluded
    from the conversation she was so intently following.
She just assumed they didn't hear her agreeing, I guess.
    Mike-who-would-be-dad took her by the hand and me
by the other and led us out of the park quietly. I knew then
    that he was a friend, probably our only one; not that
my aunts and uncles and grandparents didn't come by regularly
    to grope me and feed me shandies, but something burned
behind their eyes that precluded any notion of friendship or love.

    We got another friend a few weeks later, when mother
tried to take me across the pedestrian bridge; she clutched
    at the railing for a few steps before the thrud of cars
beneath us made her start to shake in a familiar way, and she
    crumbled slowly to the pavement, sobbing quietly
as a pool of urine darkened beneath her. Women pushed by us
    with strollers, pretending not to stare
by staring right at us as I tried to talk her into standing up.
    I had got her halfway to her feet when a woman
with a wooden bead necklace and shiny red leather shoes
    walked over to us, took her arm, and led her to the park bench
on our side of the bridge. Sissy was our friend after that for almost
    six months; I even got to stay overnight at her apartment
once in a while when mother needed a rest. Her son Rudy and I
    would eat frozen pizzas while Sissy
went out for an hour or two at a time with men who drove up in front
    and beeped—her appointments, she called them.
After I told mother about all the appointments Sissy had, her face
    went white and she told me to never
talk to Sissy or Rudy again. We moved to a new apartment
    over by the museum about a month later,
and Mike and my mother got married the year after that.
    As I watched the tail lights of their VW station wagon disappearing
down the driveway the night of the wedding,
    I knew that I had lost all of my friends,

and that it would be much harder
    to find any new ones now.

I turned and slid down the couch and watched my grandmother
    sleeping with a lit cigarette in her hand,
makeup in puddles on her face, then pulled a blanket around my feet
    and breathed quietly, knowing that it was better
to let the whole house burn down with me in it
    than risk waking her. I was asleep before the ashes fell.

When Loverman Pulls Up

When loverman pulls up in his big yellow car
she runs to the bedroom and puts on her hair
so she'll be ready to go (but never too far).

Her brother's gone out, he's slouched in a bar,
wishing she'd want him to stay, to be there
when loverman pulls up in his green ragtop car;

says he'd *cut'em good, twice so it'd scar.*
Earlier he helped her pick out what to wear
so she'd be ready to go (but never too far).

Her nose twitches when she smells his cigar,
the cologne and old jism: such romance in the air
when loverman pulls up in his dusty grey car—

Laying back, she sees lights from The Falling Star
as he comes, then pulls up her underwear
and gets ready to go (but never too far).

She puts cash in a box inside the armoire,
tucks in her son, and his teddy bear,
then gets ready to go (but never too far)
when loverman pulls up in his little brown car.

And We Moved Like Heat

School was a fight to the death, always,
a way to learn from the herd
                the ways of the herd.
We lined up in the halls and waited,
month after month, to be humiliated
by drudges who'd confused discipline
and desperation so long ago
that the only thing holding them upright
                was the color of fear
in our eyes, a thing they tended to
as though raising orchids from seed.
Month after precious month we grew more feral until
we exploded into sunlight... though there was never enough
of the first summer day's hot breath   the rec center pool
   with the little tray of water to wash
      the cut grass   from your feet
         every fence wanted climbing
   or crawling under   except when there were dogs
on the other side   plenty of brush
to crouch in   while throwing rocks at cars   or hiding
   from the tenth graders in their red chevy
      the ones whose cigarettes we stole
         from the shorts they left
           on the bench by the pool smoking and coughing
    and trying to wash the smell out of our hair in the creek
Everyone's Mom had Kool-aid   everyone's Dad
   burnt burgers on the grill   sacks stuffed with popcorn
For the drive-in the trip to grandma's
   playing basketball with a hoop
      nailed to a telephone pole
         so you had to learn where to dribble
     to miss   the potholes
running through the sprinkler
till the old man yelled,
hours that bled like water colors

into notebook paper--days that grew narrow
at the end, when we knew what was coming next,
and so we sobbed quietly in our beds
like the grownups did, putting one leg out
from under the sheets to keep cool,
listening to every dog
in the neighborhood bark at all the others.

A Glimpse of The Future

I've only to close my eyes, and there I am:

in a home for the busted, the inoperably old,
listening to Grandma mumble
about how the center of the earth
is a cave filled with dinosaurs and ferns,
headless dwarves with faces on their bellies;
how she can hear them cackle
in the hollow middle of everything—
then watching as she falls to her knees
on the linoleum, performs ablutions,
massages the beads and rocks in time
with the word.
          And because now she has names
for the voices that rise up
to taunt her, cast barn-loft shadows,
push her far back into the eye,
I kneel beside her in the day room
and remember how, when I was the child,
she used to catch me alone
and dig a fingernail into the soft skin
of my anus like she was trying
to get the last olive
from the jar.

I've only to close my eyes, and there I am.

Three That Moved Me

As will happen with young boys, my first crush
was on a girl far more developed than I
and five inches taller besides.
Ah, Laurel! The most womanly twelve-year old
ever to slap clogs on the linoleum floor
of William Gillette Elementary... On the very morning
I resolved to ask her to the Fireman's Carnival
a fly, small and shining blue-black, shot into my nose
as I walked through the bus circle.
The scene is still clear: the buzzing in my sinus,
how lodged the bugger had become,
the look on Laurel's face as I staggered into the lobby
     blowing hard enough
that the fly shot out
and whizzed away.
I wrote my first poem that night,
but I didn't mention the fly.

Then there was Myrtle, pleasantly round,
brown as a cup of cocoa--
she liked George Benson and wore shoes
that were too small for her feet
so that the skin poked out over their tops like dough.
We got so far as to make a date for the Spring Dance
before her friends found out
and made clear to her
the immorality of dating a white boy.

Ivy had no such problem, sweet Ivy
whose skin was so pale
it almost glowed—she lived up the street
with her father (who made his living
karate-chopping watermelons in half on the stomachs
of volunteers from the audience), two brothers,
and the ugliest bulldog anybody had ever seen.

We sent notes folded into elaborate packages to one another
discussing the difference between liking someone
and *liking* someone, until one day
she invited me over, Dad was away.
When I got there, brother John said
she was still at the rec center
learning how to weave leather, so he and I
swiped a half-full bottle of Jack Daniels
from the liquor cabinet and slammed it all down
in twenty minutes, so's not to taste it. Then somebody
got the idea to drop the dog down the laundry chute,
where it got stuck near the bottom
and started whining
just as Ivy walked in with a handful
of coiled friendship braids. John and I
stumbled out the back door, leaving Ivy
to get the beast free by squirting a tube of Prell
down the chute and putting some leftover hamburger
at the other end for encouragement.

That's what John told me, anyhow,
since Ivy never spoke or even looked at me again.
I wrote my next poem about her, and the dog,
and about Laurel and Myrtle and the cruel tint
that lay across the world like shade,
and about whoever it was
vandalized my good winter coat with India ink;
I wrote it on thick-ruled paper
while sitting on the foundation wall
of a soon-to-be manufactured home,
   blowing a single-note song
across the mouth of an empty pop bottle,
looking out over the treeless pocks
of the Wildherd Oaks housing tract.

Feeling More Than One

Love or something like it shuddered through us
as we lay in plowed-over fields
beside a bulldozer parked
on squares of plywood—
as the evening sun licked at our eyes
we fumbled beneath each other's waistbands,
boy, girl, it felt so similar—
we set twigs on fire and learned about smoke,
hot-wired the dozer and let it chug into a ditch,
then shivered as night leapt out
from behind the edge of the highway
and sent us hurtling home over roots,
false pockets of oily sand, voles skittering,
glass and bits of wire until, breathless
and safe, the quiet returned.
There we sat, on porches half a mile apart
watching the blue hum coming
from the old-man's yard,
waiting for a cat to leap up
and swat at the condom stuffed full
of the remains of tuna sandwich,
the one we'd left dangling in front
of his enormous bug zapper
as a lure; we sat and waited
for a noise to erupt like lightning,
a white-hot scream
meant to shatter the symphony
of snaps, buzzes, pips, and farts
lulling us toward sleep each night—

Among the Ten Thousand May Be One That Returns Us

One thickset day I rode home
    on my pre-owned tenspeed
and mother was leaning in the doorway
    with a mewling, soft-skulled
baby in her arms, a little brother for me
    to bully and to comfort.
Two years later my sister came home,
    so small we bathed her
in a mixing bowl. Mother never again
    went away after that,
never needed to rest at the state hospital,
    never was found hiding in a bush
by a neighbor, because with three kids
    there was just too much to do.

And so we managed to form a bridge
    between the world outside her skull
and the sulphurous caverns within, even though
    she'd forever straddle the gulf,
half present at Christmas dinner, half coiled inside,
    bobbing in the Lethe—she was
our great success, and it made us wonder
    about other ways to make things right--

And we wondered this as a wife and three kids,
    two jobs, and a whole feedbag full
of wild oats kept my step-father out till all hours
    drinking Cream Ale and getting head
from every waitress and barmaid that dug the way
    his mustache twitched--though
mother never noticed much, the rest of us did,
    and we hated how he made us love him.
When she was five, little sister's heart defect
    put her two months in the hospital
getting her valves scraped, which slowed the old man

  down a bit; the Saturday night
after she came home, he even took us out
  for pizza at Proietti's.
But then he slid away again: strange women
  called the house late at night
and father only came home to puke or pass out.
  It took some bad Thanksgiving turkey
nearly killing little brother to bring father back
  for good, to lay him down beside
his youngest son in the operating theatre,
  a moist, blue kidney being rolled
on a little cart from one open body to the other.

And today, even thought we know it was *E. coli*
  forced his hand, we still believe
that really it was magic, a secret message
  only we could read: *living is nothing*
but an act of worship--and then, when we are told
  that mother was given
some new drug after little sister was born,
  we smile, and listen to the story,
but even so--the sure and silent look
  given across the table spread
for yet another holiday
  says: *we know better. We know*
there are secrets no knowledge can obscure.

13

It was decided that I should have a party for my thirteenth birthday,
so my mother invited a cadre of those classmates I hated dearly

to come run on the lawn and eat ice cream cake. Cars pulled in
that morning and spilled out cruel little people one by one,

grabbing at party hats as crickets whizzed across the yard—
suddenly a Corvette screeched up and Uncle Patrick and Uncle John

piled out amidst the clink of bottles and grabbed me by the arm,
telling my horrified mother they had some surprise waiting.

As we drove out into the country, Patrick crowed again
about getting me drunk on Schnapps when I was six months old

while John grinned and fiddled with the radio. At The Falling Star
we parked on a gravel lot by the edge of a marsh. Patrick

pulled up a barstool for me to sit on and told Carl
the bartender to pour me a beer and a shot.

I was 5'7" at 13, but I didn't look anything close to 19. Carl
didn't care. They bought me 2 more rounds, and Carl

bought me one too, and then we climbed into the Corvette
and drove back to the party where my Uncles dumped me

in a lawn full of chocolate-swabbed little toadies
and roared away, leaving me drunk on the curb,

watching their car vanish around a curve. I wanted,
of course, to go with them, but instead I just puked

on Michele Pujilio's summer dress and laughed a crooked laugh—

we all knew, by the sound of it, that I was ruined. Not only

now, but for the rest of time. So I laughed again, just to see how the world shook. Like a soft-boiled egg, as I recall.

And It Never Stopped Snowing

It was Christmas eve that made my luck
Turn sour. A thirsty voice caught my ear
And brought me home, made me suck
The parched teat of another spent year

And watch beaten people drink cheap beer:
Uncle Patrick in his Post Office truck,
Drunk as god, shouting *Da Mailman's Here!*
It was Christmas eve that made my luck

Into a memory. There I was, stuck
In the kitchen, trapped by grandma's queer
Sobs, watching mounds of ground chuck
Turn sour, when a thirsty voice caught my ear

And pulled me aside: now Patrick's sneer
Was a happy one. *Well hey, you little fuck,
You look like the fag got me drunk in Korea
And brought me home, made me suck

His cock till I puked! Man, I had to tuck
Him into bed with a bayonet up the rear!
I love you, buddy.* Suddenly I came unstuck,
The parched teat of another spent year

Blowing madly into the stratosphere
Like a burst balloon. Before the clock struck
Twelve I was checking my rearview mirror,
Heading west, ready to self-destruct.
It was Christmas eve.

part 2

The First Lesson

    To know America, you must first know
its high schools. I could walk to mine and watch
       budding young tube-topped girls
pressing the pimples of shitkicking bohunks
       between their teeth
as an act of devotion, spitting to one side
       like it was chaw; later these young men
would gather at a corner of the cafeteria
       and swap furs from the animals they'd trapped
and skinned for angel-dust soaked Lucky Strikes—
       I always kept an eye out for the dealer
with the squirrel-skin hat after watching them barter
       such strange stuff. It was like every other high school,
I suppose, crammed full of future citizens,
       current criminals, and those
learning to move effortlessly between the two—
       my family moved into the district
after step-dad got a corporate job,
       allowing us to leave the apartment complex
with the brown cord carpeting
       for a manufactured house with aluminum siding
and maroon shag, all a mile
       from the school where I began ninth grade.
I got in a fight the first day,
       and most of the days after that,
as various tribes found in my spiky hair and combat boots
       just the sort of excuse they needed
to exercise their squirming hormones—
       I lied about the bruises and such well enough
that my academic career continued this way
       for six months, until one soggy February morning
a dozen members of the varsity football team
       came streaming out of the gym and chased me

down to the creek in the woods
    where they beat me 'til my eyebrow
was left dangling from my forehead. Twelve stitches
    or so later, having convinced my parents that I fell
on a bridge and split my head,
    I began stalking the bastards who'd done it,
one at a time. I made it as far as the quarterback,
    cracking his knee with the edge of a hockey stick
as he emerged from the shower,
    before the principal decided
next year's homecoming would be ruined
    if he didn't do something.

I intercepted the letter expelling me
    and had phone calls from the administration
routed to my aunt, who performed admirably—hell,
    no one cared about paperwork,
they just wanted me out,
    and so did I. The next months
were made up of days of quiet glory:
    each morning I headed out
with a bookbag full of things I wanted to read,
    and occasionally understood: Baudelaire,
Spengler, Levertov, Hume, Burroughs, Woolf, Canetti;
    I went out and down into the woods
with a joint or two and sat in the shell
    of a car filled with shotgun holes
and read and slept and jerked off and watched the sun
    glide along branches.
I could hardly wait for sophmore year.

They caught me, of course, and then we moved again,
    this time to a house on the fringes of wealth,
in a town where no one would bother beating me—
    but it was too late. Two more schools
threw up their hands, and the neighbors began to call
    and complain that my presence
was frightening children and lowering property values.

    So I quit home and moved to a part of the city
where tourists would pay to have their photo
    taken with me:
safety pin through my cheek, middle finger raised;
    I was Mickey Mouse waving from the summit
of Epcot Center. The first lesson you must learn,
    if you want to become a good American,
is to make yourself tasteless, or else
    America will eat you alive.

Get On With It

Mr. Narrator, this is Bob Dylan to me.
—D.Boon

By the grace of the pituitary I hit
six feet tall and fifteen years old
simultaneously, and with a bit of fuzz
glazing my cheek as well the fake ID
was just convincing enough to get me
past the junky bouncer and inside the bar
where The Cramps were playing. Ian
brought blue microdots, so small
I took three, washed'em down with MD
twenty-twenty in the alleyway—and so
punk rock changed my life, or maybe
it was all the acid, or else when I saw
the lead singer stick his fingers up
into the drop ceiling and yank down
at least half the tiles and then start
to club the bar owner with a bottle
I knew, sure as spit, that I would rather
rise up with ribaldry, stage flytings
and fight over beer than spend
one more day receiving the word:
this is how we behave in public,
this is how we make America proud,
this is how we excel at standardized
testing, this is how we bury our scent
under pastes, sprays and powders.
It was difficult to convince those believers
who'd invented my own best interest
that I wanted none of their *logos,*
that I was more than a little bent,
that I was plain crooked... still, I managed,
and just in time the see the word
        rising like the tide

all around me, as though an ocean
had formed from all the stories poured
into the helpless mouths of the dead,
overflowing them with the shared memory
of a golden age that never happened—
It has always been this way, of course,
all puppet and no string, so that the hand
going up my ass and making my mouth
move and my eyes roll is surely my own.
Or maybe not. The hardest thing
is trying to make it be still: a boat
with no captain. A tree too gnarled
to give shade. A thing among things.
That's the trick, the one I keep failing
to learn, and so make poems instead.

LSD Madrigal

Climbing

Though my face hurts from laughing so hard,
I can't seem to stop it from grinning,
or am I crying? My cheeks are moist and hot.

Did someone speak? Can you make a word?
The room, no, the whole world is spinning—
    though my face hurts from laughing so hard,
    I can't seem to stop it from grinning.

There's something that slithers out in the yard:
the grass itself: the world beginning
to make sense! I must never leave this spot
    though my face hurts from laughing so hard,
    I can't seem to stop it from grinning,
    or am I crying? My cheeks are moist and hot.

The Broad Expanse

When the taste of strychnine on my tongue
makes the air smell like burning glue,
I need to be somewhere else right NOW.

You made me feel uneasy, stupid, young,
When your mouth said: *Yeah, I hate it too*
    when the taste of strychnine on my tongue
    makes the air smell like burning glue

That's why I had to go hide—it stung
to know my thoughts get away, poke through
into words, that you can hear them, and how,
    when the taste of strychnine on my tongue
    makes the air smell like burning glue,
    I need to be somewhere else right NOW.

Crashing

I try to sleep but my eyes are beachballs
and they itch. A chicken screams on TV.
A word sparks in my head--then is gone.

The wriggling wall no longer enthralls
the worn-out synapses that operate me.
    I try to sleep but my eyes are beachballs
    and they itch. A chicken screams on TV.

At least we had fun, so the mind recalls
how playing at madness made us feel free.
On the short, hard hairs that bristle at dawn
    I try to sleep but my eyes are beachballs
    and they itch. A chicken screams on TV.
    A word sparks in my head--then is gone.

Staples

Neckbone, legbone, stalk of thyme,
peanut oil dregs—all the near-to-rotting bits
plunked into the broth and boiled hard—
tomato ends, soft onions, wilted lettuce, another
legbone; the sense of destroying evidence
is palpable now.
From here I can see across the street
where shiny, bulbous trucks
scoot up and deposit children
at a school bunkered beside
windows full of newlyweds
preparing for work-a-day separation
in the old paper mill they've made into condos.

So many people, everywhere,
what the fuck are they all doing—as soon as this broth
is strained and skimmed and thickened,
poured into the steam table, into the bowl,
someone will taste it
hesitantly, as a first course preceding
Rack of Lamb with Poached Asparagus,
perhaps, and they will pin their confusion
to a practiced grin and raised eyebrow. Delicious,
Truly sublime, they'll say, and then the rest of the table
will eat garbage and scraps and proclaim their love
for the human experience. Me
too.

My Hometown Is Filled With Crazy People

Dave told us he took handfuls of speed
and chanted the alphabet backwards so he'd
seem crazy when he met with the draft board.
The plan worked so well he even scored
twenty years of SSI, and on the third
of every month he got a check that covered
his rent, food, and enough sacks of ganj
to get to sleep. His skin was faintly orange
and he stank to hell. My first roommate.
Before I moved in, I'm told, he was sedate,
medicated, a graduate of R-wing—
two months later, on a Thursday evening,
he threw a TV set at the landlord
who had come to evict us. When bored,
which was always, he'd put cans of beer
in the oven till they burst; we would hear
him shout *Oh, baby!* as he poured hot ale
down into his pants. Other times, he'd flail
about like an epileptic, or just stare
for hours like some hideous cat, nowhere
and everywhere all at once. Best of all
was when we painted over the "e-r-a-l"
on the Funeral Home sign next door,
then shellacked it. That happened before
Michelina showed up one day, more insane
than Dave or anyone else—she'd complain
her pussy itched then pull off her skirt
and lay down on the sidewalk to flirt
with invisible boys—the mind of a child
in a porn star's body, and *rape is mild
when it's smooth like Daddies fist,* or so
she said—Dave was smitten, ready to go
and find a job or get back on Thorazine,
whatever it took to make her the queen
of the world. All it took was a sharp eye

and a bed. They found a place nearby
our old apartment and, well, made a home,
such as it was—he'd drink beer and she'd roam
down to Seven-Eleven looking for cock
until he could sneak up behind her and knock
her over with a bottle. That was their way.
Ten years before, when the state couldn't pay
to keep all the loonies quiet in the bin,
it was decided to let some begin
to re-enter society, let them live
among us, under strict administrative
supervision, of course (many would become
steady renters of the flop-houses, but some
built weird shacks in the abandoned subway).
Then funding for that program went away,
as the city focused on tax relief
for the business sector. In the very brief
time that Michelina lived outside hospital
before od'ing on phenobarbital,
she helped, if that is the word, to defray
the cost of (approximately) one bouquet
of flowers in the lobby of the hotel
that was built downtown to attract the well-
to-do by not sleeping in a state-owned bed.
Even greater savings now that she's dead,
I suppose, which is not to say that it's wrong,
it's just our way. Dave didn't mourn long;
after half an hour of tears he laughed
and said "She got me with the witchcraft,
that stupid bitch. Glad that shit's all over
and done." But I know you still love her,
I told him; "Sure," he said, "but--ah hell, why
worry? Only the insane are 'fraid to die."
Then he started laughing so hard it seemed
he wouldn't be able to stop. "I dreamed
her," he choked, "and I dreamed your ass too
you fucker." The lit cigarette he threw
missed me and landed in a pile of trash.

The small, gentle tails of smoke were the last
thing I saw as I closed the door; two
hours later the fire trucks came through
and woke me up in time to see flame
rising blindly above the trees. Then came
the knock at the door, the very one I'd
been expecting. "You know, I really tried
to put it out," Dave said. He handed me
a beer and lit a cigarette, waiting to see
if I was only one of them disguised as one
of us. I grabbed the phone and dialed 911
and told them all about fires and men
who could start them. Then I sat down again
and listened to Dave sobbing, his tears
cleaning paths in the soot—he didn't hear
the police at the door, didn't speak at all
as they dragged him, cuffed, into the hall
and vanished. I dreamt the look in his eye
that night. The next morning I got high
and started my new job at a factory
on the northside, a wide, brown, two-story
building with no windows except the one
in the lobby. Day after that, I bought a gun.

Maukin at the Harvest Home

Feed, and grow fat; and, as ye eat,
Be mindful that the lab'ring neat
As you, must have their fill of meat...
—Robert Herrick

The rising sun made the gull into a flash of pink,
    red glare on a white bird turning—
there were three of us watching from the rooftop,
    watching the seabird rise above the cranes and stacks;
as it dove and dipped and shone the gull became a knife
slicing through the shroud of hand-me-down slogans
    with which we'd shuttered every hole in our heads,
        letting light fall
    where light had not lately fallen:
we were young, and so believed
that through disorder we might escape
    the plots numbered for us on the far field,
that way of going down into the earth
    without disturbing the slumber of a single rock or root—

My friends on the roof:
    Marie, a painter,
        was a woman that moved like a magnet
in a room full of iron shavings, men and women both
    made hopeless by her step—
she had her canvas and brushes
to vanish into when the threat grew too vivid,
    as I had my poems and words to slide about with—
only Peter had nowhere to go,
        nowhere but her,
unable to howl or seeth unless it made her feel
            anything—
and so he became a cage and laid himself down around her,
    drove his knuckles into her face

and dragged her by the hair when he was jealous
(always).
The way it would end was obvious,
so I decided to give them something they could use:
    one awkward joining of bodies was enough
        but to be sure we tried again and again,
    waiting for Peter to find out.
He did, and the night he held me against the wall
and pointed some ridiculously smug pistol at my head
    I knew I had succeeded.
Of course he let me go,
found Marie and did the same thing:
      do you want to die?
When she answered just as I had, he sighed
and then boy didn't he show us,
    putting the barrel in his mouth so there'd be no open casket.

So that's how everybody got what they wanted:
                        she was free,
              he was free,
and I had the makings of a new career:
    like a scarecrow
that makes the farmer feel safe
    all the while pointing crows toward new seed,
        harboring mites and grubs where its leg
meets with earth, so too
    would I find meaning in seeming compliant,
                      useful to all,
    quietly letting my straw grow into kindling,
        angling my chest toward the sun a little at a time
until the flames could shoot out and set the whole field ablaze.

It didn't work out that way, of course;
    such grand designs are only the vanity of scarecrows.
Instead I sit far from those rooftops
    and think about pink birds
        turning high above the decay

of days so far gone I doubt their existence,
    fiddling with the last frayed ends
of a youth that has let out it's thread,
    suddenly unable to describe the joy
                  I feel in knowing
I shall never have to pass that way again.

part 3

How About A Little Fire?

In Minneapolis, Minnesota,
I shacked up with a toothsome, corn-fed girl
and found work making chicken fried steak
in the Mall of America. Earl
and Johnny and I would go on break
after we'd dunked our quota
of battered meat into vats of hot grease
and pass around a pint of whatever brandy
was on sale—E and J, mostly—and smoke
whatever else was handy.
They'd ask about my girl, and Earl would joke
about me going back to school piece by piece,
since Lisa was a substitute teacher.
She would never come drink at the place
they all shared in St. Paul
because she was scared of black faces,
black voices, nightfall,
coffee grinders, and sitting in the bleachers
where someone could look up her dress.
Most of all, she was afraid
of being considered anything less
than a radical feminist. So she stayed
on the city line and I went back and forth
between her and my friends
in the ghetto. It couldn't last,
of course; I would overextend
myself sooner or later and have to choose fast
between imagining I was worth
what we chose to call love
and feeling at home in the absence thereof.
Earl, Johnny and I moved well together,
since we all liked to drink and get high
and hated our lives. Earl was the old one,

still had a Jheri-Curl—Johnny, younger, would cry
when he got drunk then pull out his gun
and threaten to kill us (there were never
any bullets). I was bigger
than both of them and drank
more, faster, and got into a fight
everywhere we went in Earl's tank
of a car. I think it was Thanksgiving night
they made me an honorary nigger,
after I told them about the schnapps
my Uncle made me drink when I was six
months old. Then Earl opened a fifth
of Chivas, swigged, and got sick
right back into the bottle. I went with
Johnny to the Stop-and-Shop
while Earl tried to pour the booze through
a seive, and J told me I was
the only person who didn't look scared
first time he pulled his gun on them. *Cuz,
you are either very cool, mentally impaired,
or dying is something you wanna to do.*
I knew. The snow was falling in sheets
from an empty sky that stretched on
and on. I told Johnny I had to go meet
someone, and drove back through town
toward a house where I'd discover Lisa's gut
poisoned with a child
that neither of us wanted to bring
into this world. She smiled
when she opened the door, as though everything
would be as simple as the way it shut
behind me. Later we went and had it extracted;
made a clean break. It was the one STD we'd contracted.

Goodbye, Gentleman Farmers

Summertime in a place of deep snow
makes everyone half-crazy. My window
is propped open with a cedar shim,
and I can see dawn spreading across a palette
stacked with clay-red bricks.
A dusty Ojibwe man across the street
in a baseball hat
    pleasuring his ass
against a naked beam,
and the street cleaner shuffling by,
making things right
for the Fourth of July parade.

My room has everything a man could want
when a man wants to leave: refrigerator, stove
bed, chair, sink, chest of drawers, and all
in a space just large enough
to allow the inhabitant to enter.
It is an escape pod
primed to launch me to Chicago
and points more distant.
I slide in sideways each night,
fill my glass,
and count the days..

The hermit in the room beside mine
has a head of white stubble
and smells like bologna.
after midnight he curses at me through the radiator
in a slurred, burbling play of signifiers:
goddamnissnitchedpunkcumdrinkinfuckererer...
And after midnight I reply
by reading him snatches of Richard II
or *Batter my heart, three-personed God,*
when he pauses for breath.

 (never
have I felt so understood.)

On Saturday nights I go to see Mr. Bush
the ex-pimp, then ex-junkie, then ex-pimp
again and now smoker
of cheap cocaine. I have met
some interesting people
at Mr. Bush's apartment,
and they all cry sooner or later,
and they all stop once the stem
comes around to them and the smoke
pierces their misery and hangs it out
to dry.

Tomorrow evening I will leave Minnesota
without knowing why the shape of a day
expands, contracts, pulls us onward—
for the moment, I think I'd better
go tell the Ojibwe across the street
that somewhere in the world his childhood sweetheart
is on fire, or is happy, or both.

 (Red rose
the sun in a swaddle of cloud
as we spoke. Like a wheel it spun,
so fast it seemed to be going backward
when in truth we simply
 hurtled on and on.)

Dog, Cat, Man, Bird, Bear, Wind, Day

It's Fourth of July and the parade
    marches on, through streets thick with steam
        rising from the pavement,
from the weiners floating in pans
    of grey water, from our uncovered
        heads—how many such days
can we possibly have left? Just the one,
    over and over again. Perhaps
        at some distant place, once the age
of nations is artifact, we'll have become a lesson
    for children:
        They were not a happy people.
They cared greatly
    for sums. Their sense of time
was fractured.
        For now, the fireworks
    spit up over the pedestrian mall,
        each rocket loaded
with an amethyst spray of sparks meant
    to remind us of some lost wisdom: dog, cat,
        man, bird, bear, wind,
day. The skies fill with ash
    and little pellets of condensed proverb
        falling into the parking lot,
vanishing like first snow.
        Most of them
were snitches and mice, but a few
    managed to remain
bloodthirsty.
        First you live, then you die. Make sure
    you have plenty of blankets and toilet paper
        and ice for your drinks.
        They had
a queer beauty to them, a belief
    that everything would someday

>   *make sense. Of all their habits,*
> *the strangest was: they meant everything*
>   *they said.*
>   And even when the lies were
>   as obvious as smallpox, as shackles, as soil
> scorched and long dead, they built legends from them.
>   Not once, but a thousand thousand times,
>   till their stories filled the air
>   like spoor.

Lost In The Land of the Holy Ones

I. *Smoking Crack on the Loading Dock of Michael Jordan's Restaurant*

Ana 'l-Haqq! (I am the Real!)
—Husayn ibn Mansur al-Hallaj

After plodding through a Thursday night shift
I shot pool with Cheo the fry cook and watched
the crowd gather along the bar. Sleepy-eyed
grifters and their marks, Hooters girls, ex-jocks
nervous with steroid burn—everyone, it seemed,
but the one I craved came funneling in,
pushing the roof higher with their voices,
swapping flesh and tales of flesh. Six whiskeys
into it I fell to talking with Cecil,
who swore he'd played nose tackle three years
with the Bears and was up for most anything—
A little Prudential, perhaps, our fucking Piece
Of The Rock but both our bankrolls were slim
and thirsty. Presto! Dave the ex-bartender
comes teetering in, arm in a ragged
yellow sling, half his head burnt up and scabbed
like purple stucco. As he told us how
he got to looking that way, he flashed
a bouquet of Jacksons, said he got them
from victim's assistance. I nodded, winked
at Cecil, then borrowed Dave's good arm,
and led them both out to smoke a joint.
I lit it, smiled, and pulled hard on the tip
as a swift and ready fist drove Dave's purple head
Into the brick.
        Later, as we sat smoking crack
on the loading dock of M. J.'s restaurant,
I watched Cecil's face glimmer as he talked
about the life that didn't happen. I
lit the underside of the glass 'til the smoke

that smelled of burnt tires wafted up then pulled
gently on the pipe-stem, feeling the center
of my head unspool like yarn, each thought suddenly
voiceless, unbothered, lost in a sort of cooing—
as I passed the pipe to Cecil I knew,
quick as light, that he was an angel,
terrible and thick, and that he was not my friend—
but he was all I had, and growing to a small
and shriveled husk of a man was worth fuck all,
love, death, cock and cunt and evolution… what for,
when it's all as insignificant as I,
as useless as a fart, a brick, helping orphans
on Christmas or dunking a basketball.
I saw it written on the dishwater sky, and I saw
another, blind and bloody thing,
trying to squirm loose. To exist.

II. *A Finger Tip In The Lettuce*

There was far, far too much Friday afternoon to deal with,
and my hangover had burrowed into the tips of my teeth,
made them all a nerve—a fried bologna sandwich
and some store brand corn flakes wouldn't stay snug
in the gut, so I wiped off and headed out
across the street to work. My tendons
remembered the swift, base motions, faithful
as twine, and I chopped and roasted and felt the booze
begin to seep out my skin and mingle with the rest
of the reek. Paul, the scaly kid who started last week
stirred 30 gallons of vegetarian chili beside me and talked
about what cunts had done this and what bitch
had done that and I asked him was he from Tarsus?
But he didn't know. Cheo said he needed a hand
and I had two to give, and I figured
it'd get me away from the prosyletizer anyhow.
Ten minutes later, we looked up and saw Paul
in the convex mirror, pulling something

out of his pocket and dumping it into the vat
he was stirring—and what the hell was that?
I asked God's secretary, what did you throw
in the chili? What what he squirmed
and the boss came rolling by and we told him:
This slug made some special chili. I don't know
what the fuck you're talking about was all he said
before running out the door; we never saw him again
not even in the news, and when we poured the chili
into a new lex, we found fish-hooks and some #4
wood screws.
    I thought later about where he might
be hiding, holding his testicles in his hand and sobbing
as every stray noise became the howl he never could let out—
I began to appreciate the difficult position we had put him in
and forgot to watch the knife so it sliced through the tip
of my left middle finger. After bundling up the yawning end
of it, I single-handedly sifted through the Romaine
looking for a little pink thing, an offering, I suppose,
to god-knows-what. A celebrity tour appeared at the door,
and some faded Hollywood gladiolas listened
to the boss explain how we turned the lettuce by hand
to ensure a grit-free entry to the palate. As he led them off,
he turned to me and hissed: "Find it." I never did.

III. *Clean Underwear*

The time clock bit down on my card and so out
into 2:30 a.m. Sunday evening I was flushed,
finger wrapped and throbbing, six dollars
wadded in a corner of my pocket. I stood
in the queer stillness and smoked a cigarette,
listening to the city call to other cities
across the vast pockets of nothing
that make America great. As I stepped
off the curb there was a screech, a thud
and lights smearing as I soared off the bumper

of a brown Monte Carlo that did not stop;
I rolled as it bore down but still it kissed my wrist
beneath the front tire with a wet crunch.
As it sped off down Rush Street, I felt a piece
of an incisor drop onto my tongue,
and I wondered if this were at last
a destiny, and what a busted tooth
could possibly represent. Mother always said
I'd die in a gutter. Hell, everybody else said
the same thing, so to prove them wrong
I stood up and held my flipper-arm
in my good hand and set off down the sidewalk.
      The boys who jumped me
figured I was a drunk, I suppose; once
they set about kicking me and saw the clots
of blood on my face, they seemed a little sad
about the whole thing. Half a block of crawling
later, I reached the door of the welfare hotel
with the busted elevator where I lived
on the sixth floor between a man
with AIDS who sold flowers and an ex-con
who wore a diaper. Two-thirds of the way
up the stairs I started to fall backwards,
grabbed at the rail uselessly with my flipper-arm,
and fell into darkness. I woke in my bed,
my hand fat and without wrinkles, or knuckles
or lines on the palm. At Northwestern they hung
my hand from a web of delicate chains, each
ending in a harness, one for each finger.
The tally was impressive: six broken fingers,
two broken bones in the right wrist,
three broken ribs and a fractured eye orbit,
not to mention the stitches. I signed the fake
name I'd given with my left hand on the forms
some grey, shark-faced nurse had assembled
and walked out into another prideless dawn.
The way the early morning commuters leered
and swerved away from my mottled face

and assorted bandages made me dizzy,
so I sat on the sidewalk and closed my eyes.
Death was being extremely stubborn. I'd put out
a pretty swell spread, I thought, yet still
my invitation had been ignored. Maybe because
I had laughed so often at one who didn't take well
to being the butt of a joke. I only wanted
rest, same as anyone. I felt a hand on my shoulder
and looked up at a dead streetlight and Cecil,
grinning through his lips; behind him stood Paul,
the boy who'd made the chili dangerous,
clinging to the fringe of Cecil's jacket
like a baby animal.

"You look good, my friend,
like you ready to be sold for parts,"
he said, "like you waiting for something to end,
but you got it backwards—it starts
here, see, the story's just getting good.
Not like this one," and he tilted his head
toward the fishhook and rusty screw dude;
"His mother just found him hanging over his bed
from the light fixture. You tried that
one time—ripped a hole
In the ceiling, remember? Sure, you were fat,
but it was protocol
made you fall. Just wasn't time
for you yet, and neither is now,
no matter how you try to nickle-and-dime
your way in—that ain't how
it's done. Just ask this princess
behind me, he knew how to make me come
and swallow all the pain
and disgust he'd been swallowing the same
way for years, and he never once said my name."

And what is your name? I asked.

Then he laughed, and it sounded like
a squeaky freezer door. "Come on, man,
you know better than that. Mike
wanna be like me, dig, I'm your flight-plan,
I live in your bones,
I give your whiny ass a means to exist,
I help you write your shitty poems,
I'm every girl or boy you ever kissed—
You think you got it bad?
Why, cause your uncles made you drink
booze before milk? Cause your dad
is a non-event? If you think
I'm gonna take you away
just cause you want me to, well,
think again. But remember this: on the day—"
    —he leaned in close, and I could smell
    smoke and dust rising off his skin—
"—I do come, you're gonna lick my toes
and beg me for one more minute, one more spin
on this filthy little ball. I'm the one who knows
'cause I'm the one let you get born in the first place.
When that day comes, motherfucker,
        I'm gonna laugh in your face."

I could still smell the smoke where he'd stood,
and the sunlight clawed at my eyes,
and I felt things leave me.
That it was all a tawdry, soulless lie
I had no doubt, but still it soothed me
to know that there is no end to self-deception,
and that we can do little else but circle around
and bounce off this continuum of vanity
in feathery arcs,
    wishing only to forget ourselves
and our imagined infirmity. I snarled then
at the commuters dragging themselves
toward the El station, at the firmament
slicing through them, at the hum of blood—

I snarled and spit and rose up from the ground
and saw myself reflected in a shop window
    —and wouldn't you know it,
despite everything, I was still one of them.

Learning to Sleep Through It

She was waiting by the baggage carousel
with hands folded, already beginning to sob
and she hadn't even seen me yet.
Some new husband took my duffel bag
and leered at my busted face with horse eyes,
then took her by the arm and led
her bent and convulsing body gently away.

* * * * * * * *

The next morning, my limbs strewn like dunes
beneath a quilt so old the department store
that sold it
    is gone, it's hide
    threadworn, almost like hair
but bearing the imprint of beasts,
I watched dust bounce through light in circles,
pulling against gravity as gravity pulled against
my cracked bone. The last thing alive
    before half-sleep
    lathered my eyes
was a hand, reaching toward siftings of dust and sun.

* * * * * * * *

His chest heaves in sections.
    What funny noises, like the Three Stooges
      --she steps into the room
and starts to apologize, then can't
    seem to stop: *God I'm*

                              sorry,
  I didn't mean to cry.   *You were always
so calm. Your head...*   is blistered
and swollen.
      She smokes.   The body

burbles like mud.

*The way I tried to push you, to make you
what I wanted.*   The body farts
in reply. *My poor baby, what have I done*
The cry
      with which we are hurled
                  into light.

Hiding

I believe the only way to reform people is to kill them.
—Carl Panzram

Suddenly she was everywhere--
at the grocery store,
    the gas station; Michele Pujilio,
the little girl I'd vomited on at my thirteenth
birthday party now adult-sized, mommified,
with two throbbing children in tow and a baby
    suspended from her chest in a sling
of red nylon and aluminum bars. Always
she wore some sort of jogging suit, always
with her ponytail pulled through the back
    of a baseball hat. O
how well I dodged her--

but not well enough--in line at the Super-Valu,
not drunk enough and so buying beer, my name
    came squealing from behind: *Is that you?*
gosh, it's been years! and how've I been?
Lost in loathing for the likes of you but my mouth
    only said Fine. And you?
--*Oh, busy busy busy, you know, a soccermom's work*
is never done! Her eyes
pinched in on themselves: *Look at that poor girl.*
She could take care of that mustache
with a depilatory... the cashier
    looked over her lip at me sadly
    looked the soccermom up and down
    and pulled the small, ripe tears back into their ducts.
For how long I stared at Michele's smooth, spotless throat
I can't say, but as I did, I thought of Carl Panzram,
and of the slow, dull roar of people coming and going,
and how the only certainty is that we are too many,
and I wished that you all had one neck and my hands were around it.

Instead, like so many would-be murderers, I smiled at her
and went home to dream about blood and wake
    on a mattress moist and rough as a wound,
ready to watch the idea of the moon
spread itself across the earth

A Dead Giveaway

Not since Superman died, Carl would to say
    at least twenty times a day
when asked if he had a match. He'd lean
over, squint (PeeFree Dispoz-A-Bag™
    stuck in his pant leg
so the whiskey came out almost as clean
        as it went in),

and light the cigarette, then begin
    coughing, all so he could grin
as he bummed a smoke. At closing time
he moved like putty, rubbing on the bar
    and pushing the grime
in an oval, almost; if his mother
        called at four-ten

he'd stop and get groceries. Supermen
    did these things now and again.
Years ago, his doctoral thesis
had attacked the cult of Dionysus
    and its recent trend
toward mod-gaul criticism—but his blend
        of ambition,

lust, genetics, and the omission
    of certain inhibitions
made three wives, six kids, countless colleagues
and the dissertation board all hate him.
    The final intrigue
was that death brought no smell—no sour, dim
        tang of liquor

rose up from his skin—it was quicker
    than a thought: a small flicker
of eyeballs, one final raspy breath,

an imagined kiss, a quick glance at death
    and Carl simply was.
Sissy thought it was her fault, just because
        of how his cock

jumped in her mouth when he died—the shock
    made her crave a piece of the rock
even more. As she foraged for cash
she found a photo: Carl staring steadily
    into the camera's flash,
each eye a hole wanting desperately
        to be filled in.

She tossed it aside and rubbed her thin
    knees with her palms. "Shit. Some men
do 'bout anything so's not to pay."
As she laughed, his body spasmed, one stiff hand
    leaping, then falling to land
on her thigh. In it, twenty dollars lay.

Life On The Cube Farm

A certain lichen grows on cubicle walls,
one formed from discrete objects: photos of children
and pets, happygrams, brightly colored advertisements
and desert island cartoons. It's what catalogues presence

here on the nth floor. To the North are windows
through which we gaze at the yolk of the city,
and the hallway which leads out is to the South,
beside the management door, a few strides West

of the broken-off, two-cube island where
the Temporary Liaison for Change Process
Implementation sat while her husband lay dying
in the hospital last month. We watched the walls

of her cube grow earnest, jesus-y, morphing into
a spectra of cheaply made sunrises and praying hands—
someone said they found her asleep at her desk
one morning in February, that she must have been there

all night. The following weekend his fistula bloomed,
and she came in Monday wearing too much makeup,
laughing inappropriately loud—we scuttled sideways
like crabs when we heard her stomping down the aisle,

mug in hand, ready to latch onto any sudden movement.
By Friday she seemed perpetually drunk,
teetering, talking to the coffeepot; when she rearranged
the magnets on the Process Implementation Board

to spell out the word "greazy," heads popped up and down
above the cube walls like prairie dogs with sensible shoes.
She went out for lunch that afternoon, giggling,
and never came back. There is a new woman

at her station now, watching numbers float by
on the monitor, tentatively thumb-tacking things
up to the walls of her cube—she made a cake
for the management's birthday, and laughs quietly,

feigning embarrassment, like a Geisha. Yesterday
she popped the bubbles on a piece of bubble-wrap
for nearly twenty minutes. If she'd kept it up
any longer, I swear to God I would have had to kill her.

The Insult

The telephone rings, or it rang, once upon a time,
now it beeps or whistles, the doorbell, the alarm clock
    also are digitized
and at the church they press a button instead
of pulling on a rope—so it rings and a plane passes by
overhead, making the cheap ceramic bells painted
with a scene from somewhere in Germany
rattle in my mother's china cabinet.
It is how she must have imagined heaven:

a small cottage on a hillside and impossibly blue frocks.

Still the phone continues to bleat, yet another
human being bent on proving their sympathy
    and worth, or it could be
they want to tell her how she finally won
the lottery, some rocket fuel to blast her clear
    of that narrow pocket
wedged between poverty and oblivion—it's too late now,
you tapeworms, she's already won the gift of a lifetime:

watching the birds from the banks of the Rhine,

the sun fixed in the sky, shining a buttery yellow.

The Procession

Car after car simmers, waiting,
and in car after car we sit and stare
straight ahead.
        Then we shift forward of a piece,
lights ticking and small flags
marked "funeral" suction-cupped to each hood;
once over the railroad tracks the sheriff
waves us on past the trailer park
and the children frozen on the playground,
balls unbounced, swings silent, staring
at that first, brilliant wagon
and the hidden cargo
they've heard tell of—could be
one of them has seen the skin preserved
and waxy as plastic fruit, the dopey curl
of the lips that never set quite right,
the eyes not so much shut as drawn closed;
once we pass, that child will stand at the center
of a patch of beaten down grass, expounding,
telling all any of us will ever know
to the circle of little ears gathered
in the shadow of the jungle gym
at the edge of the park, beside the old trailer
that's half-rusted and sagging low
in the middle; one would think it uninhabited
but for the few strands of Christmas lights
that hang, lit, along one corner,
serving notice to the world
that breath is still taken here.

The Logic of Clouds

originally published in 2009 by BlazeVox Books

Stratus

Neither Here Nor There

Alexander is an astronaut with a shrunken monkey's head
tucked inside a pocket of his jumpsuit—it pokes
into his thigh as they leave the earth, a secret
bit of luck his crew mates know nothing of,
each pressed into their own upright cradle. The skin
of his face pulls back as he remembers Carnaval,
how Diana's face spread in amusement
when he traded money for the tiny, burnt skull,
how the year she loved him seemed
as boundless as the inconclusive curve
of space… he will show his charm, later,
once the booster has leapt into the sea
and the station has been joined with;
placing it on the bright, narrow shelf
above his bed, he will call Paolo,
the botanist, over to see this thing
that held them safe in a cocoon of magic
as they rose through, and over, and then majestically above
clouds. Holding the little knob in his hands, Paolo will think
how much it resembles an amaryllis bulb, and how
his grandfather may, at this very moment,
be prodding holes in dirt with a stick and thrusting bulbs
down into them, wiping his hands on his trousers,
and looking up at the blank sky, wondering
if they will be lucky enough
to see rain today.

The Anachronist

Both of the times he fell into the house
he scraped his face up good. His own house,
not drunk, just clumsy he tripped and fell,
he said, over a palimpsest. Well, not really over
but while scrutinizing one all proper sense
of perspective vanished and smack! A ragged
shingle tore into his cheek. Not a self-
destructive sort of man, just one flat-faced
and mad for hidden literatures.

The second time was Dante's fault,
La Vita Nuova and full-on sunlight conspired
to bash him against a loose downspout. It fell
like a redwood sawed halfway up the trunk
and buried a 1-1/2" #12 screw in the back
of his neck. The paramedics wondered at how
the just-visible scars on his left cheek (from
his first tumble) were mirrored by the freshly
red grooves dug by the gutter bracket
on his right, causing the poet among them
to declare: they look like wings.

We, his neighbors, tried after that
to give him the news about: god is dead,
authors moreso, intersubjectivity will keep
you vertical and aware of your surroundings.
All the good that did; rather than join our tribe
of practical folk and accept that history'd
ceased, he did what any romantic would do,
if so afflicted: he tore the house down
with his bare hands one clear night
when he knew we'd all be watching.

Revolutionary Intent and the Appetite of the Modern We

Demons, in the guise of gulls,
    approach the aesthenosphere and descend,
unbeknown to the vigilant;

    after prowling the docks for a night
they fly on, toward cities
ripe to bursting with souls and half-souls—

    now firmly among us,
they perch. Smog eats at their wing-tips,
    taxis clip them as they hunt for the breach...
    starved, they eat the bits of grain
speckling the shit of police horses. Eventually

(soon) they will wither completely
    into pigeons, darting greasily through the park,
still meaning to set about accumulating souls
        for the master

    but equally concerned
with a bellyful of bread crumbs
    and the rallies taking place daily
on the statue of the Civic Hero.

The Benefit of Yelling Off the Porch at Passers-by

Some dreary way of life and living this
turned out to be. While cash and market value
occupies the artisans, the abyss
gets pie-charted, sliced, boxed and sold to
spiritized CEOs who wear their zen
back-to-front, like a ballcap. No matter.
I've a cigar, rum, and a preachy little pen
to ward off bile with bile, and the fatter
my disgust grows, the faster the words come.
Petty? Petty. Hatred, schmatred. And lo, here
comes a jogger, drifting by slow as chum:
Hey! Philistine! You better disappear!
and my gall subsides with a sound like feet
quitting the plague ward for a sun-drunk street.

Doing the Books for the Galactic Sideshow

While the ringleader sleeps it off in a hay bale
I trapeze the double ledger
from side to side,
      dangling from the *summa de arithmetica,*
catching the *geometrica* in mid-air,
making the *proportioni et proportionalita*
seem death-defying. And in every village
the show is the same, the balance
but a number, the property of a set,
the age of our galaxy, scrawled
everywhere you look:
      there, the heat-death of our solar system
screeching free from a colicky babe,
its mouth a spool of zeros;
      and there, a few square centimeters of smoke
from the latest big bang
      hidden in the smell
wafting up from a lanced abscess: isn't it funny
how one little prick is enough to set things in motion?

And once in motion, forever
in motion: *Watch!,* as the galaxy tags its own high walls
with graffiti, *see!,* as it tattoos the inside of its own skin,
you won't believe your eyes! when the galaxy
escapes from impossibility, seeding
presence where none can exist,
      forcing whole clusters
of impossible life into being, legions of mites born with pencils
and slide-rules, their retinas imprinted with a desire
      algebraic in its perpetual
failure to elude itself: Expand. Contract. Expand.
Contract. Expand...

...and every night I measure these oscillations,

put the numbers down in the ledger, black fire on white fire,
and every night I take the day's profits,
stuff the bills in a bag the exact size and shape of God,
and blow the whole wad playing poker with the clowns.

Bucky, Near Infirm From Years Underground,
Resurfaces to Visit the Deathbed of Captain America

You got sick and I heard and came
and found all the vegetables
rotted in the fridge. The scene was holy:
the neighbors' chimes clanging,
eggplant deflated and furry…
It was just beautiful. You got sick

and everyone prayed and there was
time to pray; you got sick enough
to make them all believe it.

Well, good for you. The flowers
from the Falcon
cloyed, I left them in the bedpan.
When you were so sick I confess

I wished a time or two you'd just die,
and then, when you stopped being sick, well,

not a good joke. Your forehead—
the battles, the years beaten into it—
you, never a jokester, not a card or ham,
and sure not too funny this time—
and then all jokes stopping together.

I bagged groceries for thirty-five
years at your request, came running, found:
your ears pursed in fungusy pouches,
eyes blank and piggy, sharpened to points;
how is it you, old man, fought Red Skull
all those years just to give in,
just to swap your shield

for a sea side room and meals
in the commons room?

No matter.
All the holes are sewn or pressed
shut now. Might be
you are fighting still,
but not here. Not with us that need it.

The Nervous Bride Talks To Her Guardian Angel

Enough cowardice. No chicken
ever won the Kentucky Derby.
No chicken ever got to be President.
No chicken ever discovered uranium.

Orphans cry. Cripples. Anyone
of the tribe "God-looked-down-
and-gave-you-nothing," anyone
stuck in it. Things to do instead of crying:

Cancel the wedding, jump bail,
kite checks, head south; or, continue
just as you have been but wear
your hair up, maybe a small

cocktail flag, Denmark, or Chad,
stuck in the bun—we'll know then
to take you with us to the stars.
We'll know you ain't chicken,

that you have strength to resist
the radiation of tears. Enough.
chickens don't fly. Chickens we eat.
We know a great many ways to eat them.

The Perpetual Attrition of the 19th Regiment

We set the lamps down beside the road
and squinted back beyond the dome of light,
back toward all the bodies—the captain showed
us the map again, where we should've gone right
instead of left, how we might get back on track—
but we'd had enough of cartography,
and captains too. He didn't fight back,
so we fed his heart to the dog. Then Raffey
put his boots on and got us all walking
again, out toward the sound of running water
he swore he'd heard. After a mile of stalking
this aural mirage, we had to slaughter
him too, having noticed his kid-gloved hand
held a map, that his eyes burned to command.

The Janitor Takes His Rest

*There are some experiences that cannot withstand the glare
of public light without being extinguished*
—Hannah Arendt

At work, each day, for one hour, only,
the letters lie still in their bins, birds
sleep and preen on the sill silently,
and I sit, awake to light,
and light
comes in to me and reclines
on my cheek, on my crossed
wrists, seeps
between what makes bone bone—

for one hour, only, and then
the People in Charge
return to their harvest offices
and command me: "Up, up!"
and I get up
and work, and they
cannot understand why the sight of me
makes them itch,
why my idiot face smiling
the way it does
so drives them to distraction.

Or perhaps they know too well
the hush in which light can be heard.
Perhaps that is why
I am made the enemy,
a sodomite of sunlight,
an infidel of rest,
a sorry dreg who yet is master
of their own industry

and, in fact, of an entire economy
that never balloons or crashes—

Or, again, perhaps they only wonder
what it is that I am refusing
to tell, why I put on airs,
just who in the hell I think I am;
well, I don't know who in the hell I think I am,
or even how to begin such a weary,
flat, stale and unprofitable endeavor,
hemming an abstraction
with ever more finely spun
abstractions—what I do know
spans an hour, only,
even when the sky is darkly churning,
for thunder too is a form of stillness,
drowning out our monstrous babble,
leaving us properly cowed.

The Imposition of Appetite

Know, my little bellies, you sacks of meat
with howling mouths, of that time before
we were all filled with holes, when, complete
and without appetite we could ignore
the virtue of our shapelessness; how lies
came roaring out from god and god in battle
locked, how a storm of their sharp jealousies
pierced and drained us 'til our dry guts did rattle
with thirst. Learn how we became nothing but
holes extended, and why we swallow on
as void, begging for the temporary
corking of an ear, eye, nose, mouth-and-gut;
and then search out the river that can drown,
with love, both monkfish and dromedary.

The Triumph of Magical Thinking

In the hymnals of the anointed (and all are anointed)
the notes are no longer singular, pricks on a page.
All the books in the rectory have melted together,
the poorly jointed book shelf sagging away,
every word on every page faded to white,
every comma dissolved into snarls and grunts.

It seems at first a madness.
It seems at first we have lost
control of our minds and limbs,
but steady focus brings the most
peculiar distinctions into relief:
eyes both glazed and bright, grief
clenched in brows, the weight
as we raise our hands toward the roof,
and then: a thousand hymns
from a thousand mouths: the sigh
of a composite ghost.

'This is our world and we love it,"
We sing together, each to his own
spirit, each to his own Lord.

Regarding The Breach

1.

A pine cone smacks a tin roof and scares us,
satellites collapse and shower us with slag,
ash, the scurf of comets—in response, we build
the temple, the gulag, the gridiron, the bomb
and the bombshelter. The poem.

The king escapes, submitting to the blade,
the lake takes the fishmonger, pockets full of stones,
the priest fills a noose—but we are stuck,
you and I, unwilling to brook freedom insensate,
saved, ablated, again, for now.

Patches of scrub adrift on brown dirt,
gray rain scoring the surface of a gray lake,
the desert dryly weeping—always we are there,
parasitic, more sure of love than any beast,
more a place than any place.

2.

Beneath, above, surrounding a willow:
a map of every branch and root,
every leaf another word for itself.

We read the map, possess the tale,
and return with an opinion of trees
resembling Agamemnon's of women.

But something human forever forgets
how to read the map of ourselves traced
by soft branches in a soft wind.

3.

Bent over the grinder, the machinist
—haloed by a cloud of steel dust—fits parts-
for some distant engine of war, or what
we still call war from force of habit.

From the corner, the radio plays
the day's most popular song: *I believe
in ghosts and goblins, in the secret rendezvous,
but most of all, master, I believe in you.*

The engine will kill its untold millions
and the steel dust, him; still, it matters
that craftsmen obey, that glyphs be carved
into the handle of the overseer's rod.

4.

The skin of the earth is thin as a fly's wing
and we ride it.
All fire rages beneath, and beneath fire,
an unbelievable stone,

then up through fire again, fly's wing, cloud bottom,
space, space, space stretched
always just out of grasp,
compelling us to try. The body is a compass

pointing the way out
of itself, but we would rather ride along,
pretending our bodies were jugs
for holding distillate, and as easy to drain.

5.

A hibiscus waves
at a corner of the window:

pink mouths, white lips, throats of green.

A man sits within,
body bent away from a woman
who kneels on the floor, rocking gently.

None of them speak.
When a bee comes to lick one
flowery tongue, the man turns on TV.

A Blister Forms

Another summer made for dry-humping
has come to the colonies, the brave new world
with a different ocean on each shoulder—
another season of perpetual
adolescence, believing we are young
and self-born, weaned from all tits in vitro.
But truly we are old, old and barren,
like some spinster aunt of dissolute royalty
who's locked herself in the attic, dances
with her ball gown, hair a mat of thistle
that turns to shiny pigtails when she
prinks in the mirror…every so often
she finds and eats the rat poison she'd hidden
months before when seized with fear
and clarity, eats it till her mind
is a scorched cloud of memory, none of it
hers, then pulls the window open
and hurls plates and saucers and cups
down at the children who've gathered
to watch and laugh and wait for flames
to lick out should she kick the lantern over,
waiting to loot the burning home and then
flee, off to guard their own dry houses
from fire. Most of them have forgotten
how the old maids' family first arrived,
fleeing some other, distant blaze, arms laden
with hat boxes and bargain china. But then
why should they be expected to remember,
since they are young, and virile, and know summer
for what it is: the season for making
furious, stupid love in the back seat
of your car, or daddies' car, anywhere
at all, never mind that it's your sister
bucking beneath you, that what you crave most

is the feel of your brother exploding
inside you, making children that will some day
ignore you, and perhaps let you envy
their own brutal summer, their own sleek cars.

USA: Two Views, 2003

How the World Sees USA

Ethnic slurs and cartoon balloons were
clever as Sammy got,
and his heart was made from a big bass drum
that marched us, day after day
down into the goddamned dirt, one way
as good as another, onward, down.

Someone made him boss and loosed him on us.
Half-witted, gospel drunk, built to drone;
he was sorry he wasn't at the other end
of the equation, since he'd so love
to worship, and be worshipful. No luck,
instead, a character as much
fastidious as beshitted. None of us
ever loved or missed him much.

How USA Sees the World

So now we're at war, and the young girls still
unfurl from convertibles their golden hair
on their way to the mall, the movie, anywhere
that sweaty-palmed boys await the thrill
of pairing off in corners, hoping to bring
a nipple to their mouths—promises are made
and sealed with spit, but true love's known to fade
when to their panties girls devoutly cling.

Later, on a hill above the internment camp,
while the boys throw bottles over the fence
at the A-rabs, a mist, yellow as old lace,
will settle down upon them all, making damp
the golden hair; by morning, boils, immense
and leaking, will have colonized every face.

Death And the Soccermom

When my spirit was overwhelmed within me, then thou knewest my path. In the way wherein I walked have they privily laid a snare for me. I looked on my right hand, and beheld, but there was no man that would know me; refuge failed me; no one cared for my soul...
And thou alone knew me as I know myself. Promise me,
    O precious one,
Promise that you will remember—
Even as { Preston / Troy / Justin   Wyatt / Jordan / Ryan } 's nose is running onto his lip,

Even as { Brittany / Tabitha / Morgan   Deirdre / Cassidy / Porsche } shrieks cause the cat

got her scuncii,

Even when you hear nothing from The Baby
(and what a bad sign that is)—
Remember, Soccermom,
      the love I have for you,
  the sweet burrs
curling up from the tip
  of my desire
As it grinds against time and I wait and I wait—

    Shed light into mine eyes, O Soccermom,
    shelter me with grace;
Give yourself to me when the microwave dings,
When the breakfast burritos slide from the tray
And { Bill / Kirk / Bob   Thomas / (never / Tom) } no time for breakfast,

And so you begin to wonder:
    why is he in such a hurry to get to work?
    why doesn't he find me attractive anymore?
    why is someone screaming in the bathroom?

did $\left\{ \begin{array}{c} \text{Jill} \\ \text{Janey} \\ \text{Jennifer} \end{array} \right\}$ order the fall sweaters or not?

Is MY MOTHER dead?
    what time is it?   O precious one,
The time for such worry has passed—

The time for swerving up the subdivision to the end of the road so that
    the kids can get the bus, for slurping your Slim-Fast in the stasis of
    traffic, for striding through the door of Macy's ready to kick ass if
    those sweaters didn't get ordered is over—

The time for wandering through Bed Bath and Beyond on your
    lunchbreak in search of tissue cozies, for daydreaming about
    George Clooney as Batman, for cutting your eyes at the horrid old
    woman returning gloves who demanded to see the manager is over—

The time for soccer practice, band practice, french club, KinderPhonics,
    fencing class, field hockey games, PTA parent-child mixers,
    creative assertiveness training and play dates
    play dates play dates has passed...

That time is gone and who has stayed at your side?
Who whispered sweetly to you

on the afternoon $\left\{ \begin{array}{c} \text{Bill} \\ \text{Kirk} \\ \text{Bob} \end{array} \right.$ $\left. \begin{array}{c} \text{Thomas} \\ \text{(never} \\ \text{Tom)} \end{array} \right\}$ and $\left\{ \begin{array}{c} \text{Jill} \\ \text{Janey} \\ \text{Jennifer} \end{array} \right\}$

called laughing from
    every champagne-soaked
        California convertible

                they could find?

Who stroked the hairs of your neck as one by one the children announced
    how they despised you and the horror you'd made of their lives,
      each in   their own special way?

Who has loved you perfectly, Soccermom?

And even if none of it ever happened,
Even if your days had splayed out according to plan
    and Soccermom lived as everyone's
        shoulder,
    breast, and warm, moist mouth,
        then who,
Who shall be with you as your lids grow heavy,
    heavier than they have ever been?

Put your trust in me, Soccermom,
And your praises shall be sung:
    on high cliffs your face shall be blazoned,
    across the desert will come the words of a song
    that tells of your many triumphs,
    the oceans shall carry your name aloft
And embroider the beaches with the sound of it...
Now gather thyself in troops, O daughter of troops,
Now lead the armies of righteousness against the enemy,
Now, Soccermom! Hold the devil's head up for all to see!
In sickness and in death! For she is my shepherd!
Ride hard live free! She setteth me upon high places!
Ana 'l-Haqq! All you need is love!
Now, Soccermom! Now!

And why? Because I too am a Soccermom,
Of a sort: harried,
    unappreciated,
        vaguely disappointed in my lot—
    Never will I lie down
In green pastures, no still waters mine to rest beside--

But I have you.　　　　And I have been with you
　　　from the beginning,
　　　　whenever YOUR MOTHER called you fat again,
　　　　when THE BOY'S mealy fingers went under your skirt
　　　　　　　　　　　　　　　after the prom,
　　　　when YOU rolled up the windows
　　　　　　　of your Range Rover and screamed
and screamed and cried and felt stupid because you'd no idea why--
I knew.　　　I sleep beneath your window.
　　　I lie between each breath and whisper
Your name, the one I knew before you were born, Soccermom.
No one will ever show you lovingkindness the way I have.
Not God.
Not even Batman.
Once you have felt my kiss
I promise you will forget all others--
　　　make haste, Soccermom, bring your lips to mine--
And now shall mine head be lifted up above mine enemies round about me; therefore will I offer in the tabernacle sacrifices of joy; I will sing, yea, I will sing praises...

The Mower Obeys The Covenant

The grass keeps on growing,
and I keep on mowing,
but sometimes I stop and I cry.

The carnivals come
and the cancer creeps up pantlegs
and lovers draw their curtains
and go about their days.

The grass keeps on growing,
and I keep on mowing,
but sometimes I stop and I cry.

I work, I follow the covenant;
I am a homeowner and a responsible
digit. If only they knew
how I longed for a sea of blood.

The grass keeps on growing,
and I keep on mowing,
but sometimes I stop and I cry.

Later, I go the food court.
Later, I watch the carousel
turning, a galaxy of fiberglass horses
collapsing too slow for the eye.

The grass keeps on growing,
and I keep on mowing,
but goddamn I wish I knew why.

The Noggin

In Which A Divorced Professor Of Marxist Theosophy, Recently Relieved Of Teaching Responsibilities Under Questionable Circumstances, Wakes From A Nap To Find His Body Atrophied And Limbs Shrunk To Flippers Even As His Skull Has Grown To The Size Of A Volkswagon, or, A Really Good Head Gives His All.

1. Suddenly Among Them

(the Professor deals with his wretched situation the way any good citizen of the modern age would.)

Early on, the headhunters called
hourly, quick-lipped herds in my ear. Want you.
Want want want you, not
proverbially, but
as a verb, a transaction, supplier
of good percentage. Then nothing but raw, gaping
      quiet, and how
the phone squats on its ledge,
leering at me. Satellites tumble
in the dark above, shelling every house
but mine with words and phrases
  of love
and desire. So,
           happy, stomach beginning to cowl,
I swallow air, fart it out again,
     stare at my tie
curling on the floor like a turd.
       I am
very nearly no one. A thought
comes pink and sluggish: so this
is success, close enough to truth
     it makes my jaw ache. Then it goes by too,
  and so

I try to turn on TV. My hands.
What have I done with my hands.
I try to turn on tv.

2. The Product Speaks

(having learned to manipulate the remote control and telephone with his strangely shriveled digits, the Professor seeks fulfillment through distance purchasing.)

This special admixture, made into foam,
infused with hand-crafted air and forced
through a very special machine
will heal you, says the head that is off screen
but must be around somewhere as
    I can hear it. This blend,

this cream but better than any cream,
this made thing made for someone like
(yes) you is exactly balanced
so it could go into your mouth
and taste just like the inside of your mouth—
    but don't put it there (disclaimer).

God it's good. Then the head appears
ready to serve, what teeth! What a gleaming hunk
of Thing-Amongst-Things! Everywhere
has a mouth, this we know, but here it is,
the mouth that can fit within the mouth
    of everywhere, make

silk of words and every birdcall you can think of. Says
the head: I will run on the feet of your dreams,
and I will make a better place
even more hyperbolic
than ever before, although, when
    our forefathers hunted elms

with their short, perfect tongues, well,

we all know how hungry everybody wasn't,
if they only worked hard enough.
Duty is elegant. The head vanishes,
the season passes, the cream arrives
    and begins to work its miracle

on the cracked and wrinkled membrane
between my eyes and what is, or at least
what seems to want so badly
to exist. It whispers when the lights go out.
It says: ah blood of my blood, I feel you, I feel you
    the way a bell waits to be struck.

3. Product Refutatio!

(the Professor experiences a strange allergic reaction and is plunged into depression after applying a mysterious salve recently purchased on an infomercial.)

And why not just be a head? Who says
the crowd must find at podium something
natty and well-limbed?
Hat-makers, that's who. Barbers. Spray-on hair
hucksters.
Once they see that this head's got
    more fingers, more knees,
        thighbones, nipples, more genital umphh
A-dangling, swaddled in curtains of cilia,
than any customer could ever

comfortably hope to entertain, well, then,
they will have no choice but
to acknowledge that I, head,
spine-guts-and-poop-hole, have tasted
    what is

    the real
    and know, as the tongue
knows, that we are a place the blood only rests upon

without piercing,
knows that we are where it sings
and sleeps, knows though I am undressed and smiling,
    reflection a guillotine gleam of teeth.

4. Cranial Epilogue

(the Professor, in reaction to media coverage of the destruction of the World Trade Center, seeks to recover a sense of citizenship by engaging in one of the few remaining Great American Myths.)

I was feeling bad, man-o-man it was an unholy funk
to be bobbing in: me, de-jobbed, friends all gone or defective,
A-rabs falling from the sky,
    sheep disease. Sheep Disease in the Promised Land!
So I clamped all the windows shut and packed up my salves
and drove 'til the gas was gone—my car
on the side of the road I walked and ran
    toward the flat puck of light
where planes were lifting
slantwise to the sky. My hand, I, with the first ticket
    anywhere (the money I had left),
in line and grinding my teeth,
felt the world return to me in a wash,
felt my people smiling at my upright brow,
welcomed the thought of cold fingers
in my rectum, how
Bomb-Free My Innards! How Conjoined
    The Bones of Me, How Noxious
To Evil is The Sweat of My Fathers!
        We taxied.

So here I am, the head extended,
new arms and legs telescoping out
on the sidewalk of somewhere
in my USA. Utah? The salt in the air.
I rub more cream into the scene before me.

    A man can become
the landscape here,
find fingers beneath the dirt,
    wake useful and in need of eggs and toast.
A nice bench, this. Good iron. American wood. Strange
no one can see me, that no one looks into my mouth,
no matter how long or loud I yell,
and don't let them touch me, no, never that.

Nimbus

In Praise of the Plague, That It Might Be Pleased and Spare Me, and My Family

O bacillus! Sacred third
aspect of the trinity,
laboring always, undeterred
by the hubris, the grave stupidity

of your various hosts—as if your survival
meant less than that of the flea, the rat,
the Vicar, the Lord! You, whose arrival
at the edge of town sends every bureaucrat

and bellboy scurrying home to seal their keyholes with wax…
Why, you are as the titans of old, your stride spanning nations,
tens of thousands laid low for your supper, leaving great stacks
of rind in your wake—and then—tired of such migrations—

you sleep the sleep of giants, of legendary things,
a sleep that hides your bedding deep
within our bodies till your greatness sings
no more. Now we live as if to keep

the old dirge from being sung,
the necrology from being read;
how quickly will we find a tongue
when the giant wakes and lifts his head?

As quickly as we'll find our eye
for spotting buboes on the street,
as quickly as we'll specify
the price our children fetch as meat.

The Tyranny of Species

They've got photographs,
the widows, pressed in sleeves of plastic.

Each hair is casually strewn
about the crowns of the heroes
and the widows too. We all get

to be on TV. We all swear to love
the baby jesus like he was our own.
During the moment of silence
old Charly whispers to me
*Ah hell, I remember
when a buckskin jacket
was all you needed to get laid.
Well, I heard about it anyhow.*

There are, as well, candles
twitching and swirling vestments
and a bake sale going on
outside the gymnasium door.

We are all on TV and loving
every minute of it. That young woman
I'd swear is making eyes at me.
Guess her dead man really is dead.
I oughta go help that young woman,
tell her about how widows are shims
that civilization uses
to balance itself,

and that balance
is a great big bug
with silent green wings.

The Tyranny of Loved Ones

After the rain-warped restraining wall broke
and dragged the men and the scaffolding down
to the unset floor of the new sewer pit,
the concrete they'd poured along the wall hung,
shivered, shone, and then detached
with the noise of an overlong kiss
before sagging in on itself and on them.

There was a sudden lack of clatter.

All at once the site bloomed with noise
as the truck crew moved to rescue those buried below.
Fire trucks and police cars and a crane converged
where helicopters already hovered, and a cage
was lowered toward the stew of support beams
and dirt and concrete and bodies. Three men
still breathed and were lifted away.

At the lip of the pit they scrounged for names.

The dead were announced, and the concrete still
shone, and the foreman swore they'd not be interred
at the bottom of a settled solid waste retainer,
but how to halt the seizure of moist rock?
The engineer claimed that sugar would stop
the setting of concrete, and so they hurried off
in a panel truck toward the supermarket.

"Sugar, damnit, I need sugar!" the foreman yelled
at a cashier grinding a chiclet. "Aisle
twelve," she replied, and the men in their boots
and their shrouds of drying mud stumbled off
to plunder the shelves.

"You gonna pay
for that?" another cashier asked them
as they rushed the door, arms laden; "Pay?
Don't you understand? The eternal rest
of our friends depends on this sugar!"

And so they poured the sparkling grains down
and halted the hardening mortar.
And things were sweeter for a time.

The Tyranny of the Firmament

The mid-afternoon people divert their current
around the half-eaten sparrow on the sidewalk,
the skull picked clean, belly still swollen with mites;

like so many of us here in the underworld
it is a thing half dissipated, half near bursting
to reveal what's consuming the rest of it.

But rather than allow the skin to crack, the mites
to gush out like froth, we cast great bones
from glistening alloys, drape them with a membrane

of polymer and rivets and launch ourselves
up toward the roof, our silver arcs and tails
of smoke shuttling toward the blue bunting

draped there, and then on through layers of black
raiment and parasol, all perfectly speckled.
The hope is that we might discover our world

lies under nothing, that the fabric of space
is endless and thus we ourselves must be whole,
as the greatest part of self is what extrudes—

everyone says so. Just ask the rumpled drunk
standing now over the bird carcass, twitching,
yelling, the one with Tourette's syndrome

and no medication but wine and the need to tell
the half-sparrow: *Fly! Fuck fuck fly! Fuck! Fly!*
Ask him, and hear, at last, the answer of a true poet.

Variations on the Theme of World Domination

Variation one: A man with his crotch
on his face. As people gather to watch
the freak whose penis, gonads, thigh-
crease and coarse clump of hair sit high
on his forehead, agents can circle around
behind the crowd and cut them down,
one at a time, quietly. Variation two:
Moral soda-pop. Easy enough to do,
if manufacturing's your thing: make
sugar-water, bottle colorfully, take
truckloads to the sweating locals. When
they raise the tincture mouthward, then
agents can circle around behind them
and steal their crop, a few tons at a time,
quietly. Variation three: Holy of holies.
The old standby. Eternal souls, knees
a-scabbing. Folks never seem to tire
of being called 'folks', but they require
a father figure to make it work. Though
incompatible with crotch-on-face, can grow
to assimilate moral soda-pop; if so,
will form a phalanx of faux-populist bent
brutal enough to quash any dissent.

Making Much of Time

These ladies must have pillows,
And beds by strangers wrought;
Give me a bower of willows
Of moss and leaves unbought
—Campion

No, no, the ring heightens the pleasure, boy,
its bite is meant to help you find the joy
manifest in pain; it helps me too, of course,
keeps you in a manly way once the source
of your sanguinity's been forgotten.
Don't cry; I too was an ugly, rotten,
spoiled little snipe once, thighs shut so tight
not even a flea could wriggle in quite
far enough to snatch a bite—but then I met
the sweet-tongued charioteer, and he set
me straight about men and women: how each fat
finger, each gnawed and broken nail that
shone pink through the cracks, even the moist, white
centers of both my palms could excite
him; and as his lips grazed from each to each
softly, well, yes, I believed he could teach
me things about love. And so he did,
and so I know: that to endure, we must bid
for the right to cause one another such
pain as human love is; that its touch
is craved by all; that with practice, your
nails can grow hard and sharp—before
long, you too will understand, my sweet:
See? Even now your joy drips on the sheet.

The Pinup Girl, Later

The phone is a princess phone, bespattered
with tears and frighteningly dormant as all
her so-called friends have forgotten about
her birthday, the tenth anniversary
of her divorce, her time of need…all these years
and still the gap's raw where he'd been,
that space he'd jammed himself into
just so he could hack away at the walls
'til their life together was a cloud of dust,
a dust that soon drifted down on the frosted hair
and attentive tits of Rigid-Tool's Miss May
Nineteen Ninety-eight. Bastard. Alimony
is all you ever were, she thinks, a way
to get the country so far outta the girl
no one would recognize me back home.
And now there's time for more acting classes
at the community college, for what-
ever… she sips her brandy and winces
at the static charge oozing up from her
center. *I've become a catalogue
of all those things I swore I'd never be:
Common. A cliché. Well, at least
I'm in California.* With one french-cut toe
she pushes the phone slowly toward the edge
of the table until it teeters there the way
the Chevy Malibu with the suitcase full
of, what was it, diamonds? had, as she screamed
through the denouement of her only feature,
the one they still show on late-night TV.
As she reaches for the remote the phone shrieks
and she stares at it, perched there, wobbling
with each ring, rocking on the table's edge…
She puts the side of her face on the teak
and watches it jiggle, waits for it to fall,
sucks in her breath and holds it:

four rings, five, ten, silence. One french-cut toe
gives it a shove, she lets her breath go
to the sound of metal and plastic
meeting tile. Must have been mother,
she thinks, fills her glass again, and walks out
into sunlight, swimming pools, her neighbor
planting tulips, the crumbling edge of the continent.

A Conceit For Middle-Managers

I just know you're going to breed, or have done,
you bed-tanned deck-hands of industry;
below deck your wife will pinch out a son
or future wife–well, *que sera, sera*–
and as soon as the little mewler comes,
you'll point at the stain on the floor and tell'em
"That's where I was born," then teach him his sums,
karate, French: cram his cerebellum
so full, the story goes, that one day he might
clean the captain's quarters, or even take
the helm when some mate falls ill. I just know
you'll bring him portside some calm, moony night
to see all the ramshackle rafts, the wake
churning up bodies whose eyes glow
like lost treasure, the thirsty moans rising
from the ones without sense enough to die,
and I know you'll show him then how to piss
like a man, over the rail, chastising,
all the while, the shipless for their sloth. "Why
don't they just get on board?" Ah, child. You'll kiss
his innocent head and wonder, at dawn,
where in the hell all the rats could have gone.

The Last Request

The three of us—two sad as dogs
(halfway, then, to true sadness)—grew
convinced under the smoke-blacked
rafters. The one laid out
was convinced and convincing both,
eyes waxed shut, hands pressed
one on the other, marzipan lips;
her wish brought us here, and we came
and stood and looked at her body
and became convinced of that particular
dead-end, that cliff bottom, the little
quiet splat all our widening bottoms
were headed for. She doffed her body
and was convinced
we would follow through,
would get her into this old, scorched,
spent shell of a church, and lay her out.

It came to rain, finally, and we two
stood and watched it hit her, watched
it peck at the hole we'd dug, looked up
through the holes at the grey cast.
We rolled her into the earth and stood
and stared. Still taking up space.
An hourglass emptied of sand. A future
rhizome, if lucky. A debt we were paying,
and the smell—
wet charred wood, funereal fluids,
pasture the next field over—was
the smell of service, and it made us
half-sad, not as though we'd loved her,
but because we could not bury her again and again.

In Praise of Breast Implants

Thanks be to Dow, thanks be Heyer-Schulte,
for taking those first tiny steps
(inshallah) toward more freakish fashions
and tomorrowland: boobs
that bend like bananas,
that meet at the nipples
in a loop, aureoles of neon
and repurposed moles
(sprezzatura!), perhaps a field
of little mouths carved all along
the downward curve, mouths
that can kiss back, men and women
both, body plastic, body putty,
body as culture metric and then—
Horror! Fashion shifts, the natural look
ascendant, culture presses down until
all the implants and add-ons
squirt out in little lumps,
landfills a-jiggle, mountains
of discard shuddering like aspic...

Praise be to Dow, praise be Heyer-Schulte,
give thanks for the future of our species,
and for its brevity. Who among us could live
with the pleasures of a finite body? Who
among us could survive
nature unmethodized?
Not that dotty grandma, standing
by the buffet table,
body shrinking but breasts
pointed at God like a tuning fork, and not I,
tapping a few lines about her
before shooting them across continents
on the electric rail...

In Praise of the Hummer

O mighty mighty, O big-ass truck,
make every errand instantly
that of a fool—and one of means,
one made O so mighty mighty,
with a ladder for to ascend,
with a ladder for to climb down,
with the slitted windows
of a medieval castle, turned
sideways—the chain of command
runs smack through the cab,
extending in either direction:
first, plastic soldiers set melting
by the heat of ignited and stolen
deoderant, then on to the rape
of puberty and the well-nigh
endless adolscence that followed,
on through beer vomit and porn,
on through the golf apprenticeship
flanked by the job your head
is shaven for (so mighty mighty),
all the way down the wedding aisle
and through the delivery room,
terminating, here, in knuckles
made white from clenching,
in the dispatches sent by radio,
as you plunder down roads
too narrow, of shoulder
too shrill (when the tires come
upon them)—but how well
they might hide thine enemies!—
until the oasis of parking lot,
the moment of serenity before
the next sorty is launched,

defenseless, and the more bravehearted
for it, into the grocery store.

O mighty mighty, we give thanks
for making clear as any blackshirt
where the fifth column stands
in the war against the Everyone Else.
(once the oil is gone, we can
cut the tires, and make of their shells
excellent shantytowns.)

In Praise of the 128 oz. Porterhouse Steak

Fleshy fingers, great fat unto the bone,
grind upon it and make it pap.
'Tis eight pounds or thereabouts!
'Tis muchly meat and what is deserved!

Two pounds in, all taste has fled.
All mouth is meat. Two pounds more
and the spine is creaking. Lick the bone,
take a rest. Beer tastes of sand.
Light like blood. Like God himself.

Six pounds fully masticated—
don't stop now. Time's bent
like a spoon. Chew. Chew.

Three bites more and glory.
Two bites more and certain Death.
The last bite placed at the top
of the alimentary canal, a flag
on an Everest of beef, a cherry
on a sundae of steak, an end
to one craving, the start
of another. We are but tubes
through which things fall,
and then we pick them up
and drop them through again—
Rest assured, there is another hole.

Christmas Market Afternoon

I pause to lean against my cart and watch
the glut of holiday shoppers seeping
every which way. Strange; there's no excuse
for how we treat each other–how, in a fit
of shopping, we might bite, claw,
scratch, steal, and scream, all to celebrate
the Rule of Claus–but still, I can't muster hate
or even disgust for a single face.
So many faces. And each one a place
beauty's born unto, each one
falling away from itself toward the day
when no one will be left to count the hours
'til Christmas, when every wall
has crumbled and all human shadow
disappeared into full light... a day for trees
to study trees, for grass to play at grieving,
and water wash itself away. Perhaps
things will be better then. Perhaps without
the glare of every human face
there will be no need for these miracles:
how we love, how we torture one another,
how we build cities in space and holy days
in time. But most of all, how we love.
Alien archeologists, take note:
our every artifact, from stone axe
to satellite, fell from this single mold.

And That, My Friends, Is The Afterlife

There are children here, performing furiously
the duties of children, and taller ones
bending the white-hot wire of later youth
into crude arcs and filaments, and of course
there are the overgrown fields of the old
and the prematurely aged... there are
a thousand animals as well, lazing
on beds of sap and musk and leaf-rind;
there is earth below, sky above,
and water threaded through everything—
and all is formed from a single element,
suspended within itself like unvarying amber,
nearly perfect in its uniformity of field
but for a tiny piece of grit at the center,
a single, static, unimaginably dense
fleck of perfect incomprehensibility:

On Donating A Kidney

On each knee sits one of the many
instances of perfection I'm party to:
a niece, a nephew, curious, both made
from fused bits of your wife, you,

and even a little of me. To make
another life is perfectly human, though
I've no need for it (too many! We are
too many! How selfish to say so)—

there are children enough here to love.
The smell of cut grass weighs
on the lawn, is drawn into their lungs,
circles, departs—but oxygen stays;

sifted loose from CO_2, it rides
blood cells round their brains
and perfect bodies, all while your gut
filters waste from ichor, strains

it pure with the organ I gave,
and was so lucky to give, to you.
My machine helped your sperm
to leap and dive. I can live through

you as well as you through me: those
children bouncing, each on a knee,
wear a trace of my shadow. Perhaps
oblivion, too, is a question of degree.

The Party Begins

The lamps in their windows and the night outside,
leaves unswept on the path, its gray stones—

from the rooftop we look out over
the cities' shallow breathing,
the way it pants with spotted lungs. Each
careful brick, every proudly curving
balustrade is shot through
with the greed of smooth beasts;
we have built, we build, an organ
designed to reject its host. In the dip
between hills our nest drips with tar.
Ah, it glittereth, yes. From fear we send
lights winking back at stars
both living and dead. And so, we dance.

A fly darts down a stovepipe.
Rain begins somewhere hidden.
Te deum. We will never have enough mornings.

He drifted up the path toward us
in his long black suit and ridiculous hat,
up toward our rooftop and umbrellas. We hid.
He knocked, then called out for anyone,
at home or in his breast; I would have
giggled, but you shushed me. When at last
he turned back, shambling down the path,
you threw a cupcake and knocked his hat
off into the brush. That's how he discovered:
the door unlocked, the stairs well-lit
and filled with the odor of wine and cinnamon,
you and I waiting to dance a circle of three.
We know his name, of course, and that
we must leave with him at first light,

wherever he would take us. Until then,
well, the roof is well built,
and dawn, inevitable. Music!

Young Mothers Aboard the Train

Their voices throb slow and hoarse.
They keep their children by an arm or collar
and talk how best to keep a house.
A word here and there growls above the rest,
the subway rattle drowns out others,
but they've no need to hear distinctly,
the question they ask one another
always the same: in all this mad, sour,
grunting world, are there none worth loving?

One still wears her high school jacket, or else
her old young man's, bangled with patches
and dark outlines where patches once were.
The other brings no feature to bear
save a long, slow sag, a watercolor rendering
of gravity. Their voices throb slow
and raw and heavy with sweat, they yank
their children by an arm or collar,
and talk about losing their homes.
They talk about girls can't keep it
together, about boys and jail, always
asking the same question: is all this mad,
dim, broken world, are there none worth loving?

Watching them, I, with my home
and husband waiting to hear about my day,
wanting, unbelievably, to hear about my day,
can only clear my throat, shift
on the thin plastic seat, and continue
listening to their song, so low, so full
of what's beaten down but keeps rising,
of the furor with which they guard
their children, of the bottomless murk
our question keeps peeking out from: in all
this stupid, careless world, are there any

worth cleansing in the torrent of love
we each manage, just barely, to keep
from gushing forth and drowning the world?

To Lie and Wait

I do not aspire to the condition
of music, or to be a little world,
however cunningly made; I'd rather
be a pediatric cardiologist
or night-soil farmer, something both useful
and along the heart, or at least along
the alimentary tract. But instead
I'm born of a man, red-haired and six feet
in length, who thinks me the product of his
noble mind's last infirmity, a song
to give others pause as the age of words
grinds itself into paste. We are at odds.

Poor sap. He thinks only about rhythm,
about how an alliterative swell
of sibillants oft melts the reader
clean away, how the honk of gutturals
riding shotgun to be-nasaled vowels
is all the reason any spirit needs.
I only want to measure the thump-thump
of little hearts, not change the way they beat—
he even suffers from the delusion
(shared by children and idiots) that rhyme
separates us from primordial slime
and makes lyres of us all. What a pity that
I possess all the relevant knowledge
of a centuries old map, since we both
are thus thwarted: My aspirations to
functionality, his hypnagogic
spirituality bound together,
useful only for keeping his time whole,
collaborating on our small, steady
extrusion until that lucky day when
his six foot length ends the life of some poor,
unwitting, eight by four by six foot hole.

In the meantime, we must keep exploring
all the oddly fjorded wrinkles
of the mind, and the world it watches
for God knows what—all in a time, a place,
has no truck with exploration, instead
preferring to suck its own teats well dry
so as to mewl about malnutrition
more convincingly. I'd never have thought
so many would feed, sob, sleep, sob, and seek
to die, all for want of what's voiced meekly
here, and in stronger voices everywhere.
Still, I am, and so have no good complaint—
that the world should have sound, smell, taste, texture,
and the brilliance to keep the eye amazed;
now that, sir, is a genius I can serve.

On the Fermentation Of Grains And Other Things

Vodka. I'll tell you why the men
sleep in their boats, womenless men
whose pillows buoy the spot: the dreamed
spot: I'll tell you: vodka made
their houses come down before ever a timber was laid.
There was a time daffodils and fruit-drowned cakes seemed
to bow beneath them, the men
with boyish lips pouting, now each a sot
and sea-ridden. Womenless, cloying, sweet at the core
in the worst of ways. The women, less from some kinder lot
than of fogs, never tell: there is no ocean anymore,
there is no river, not
even the little water, not
a single drop. But in their cups the men persist
in a drunkenness untouched by drink
while the women mutter and brandish Christ
at the docks. There is no vodka, what you feel

is a dream—but even as the voice cracks,
they wake, stomp across the deck, herds
of men come to occupy the earth or else to feel
the hatred of a drunk woken mid-dream;
they fumble toward the dream of women, the touch
of whispered hair, of the forearm, the need for a numb
and raging love, settling instead
for the sum-total of oceans: clutch
your brother like salt to the tongue: and if what comes
to greet you is you, then, by God, you've made a match.
Not that it matters; what comes
to fetch them at last will not invite itself in,
all told; womenlessness gone, manlessness

disappeared, success
masquerading as a good night's sleep, it lifts the latch,

(in its way of lifting), stands moist and, shaking,
begins
to count the liars, start them waking:

Vodka. Christ. Motion. Love in the way of simple towns.
Make yourself comfortable, it says, thrash about.
Dignity is how clowns
reproduce, so let out
your melon bursting biceps, your hair-shroud,
your face and dimples and eyes like a thirst;
make the universe something proud.
Unless, of course, you'd rather die a drunk, or a monk,
(if they be two);
unless, of course, your volume's already dispersed,
returned to cloud or fled
into the greatness of earth, and dew.

At the Lake In Wintertime

On the edge of a lake bed at low tide
between curls of driftwood we find
deer tracks in the sand. Their shape
is perfect, tapers of flame deepening
at the tips—such beauty, and then
it occurs to me how much they look
like the logo of a natural gas conglomerate
whose ads I've seen since childhood.

Now your face is the only beautiful thing
in the world, and should I look away, I'll see
that the lake bed is littered with broken bottles,
plastic bags, refrigerator parts and tires,
and that the lake itself is a silty blue puddle
of mill run-off, boat oil, and shit.

Lunatics Held In Isolation
Hallucinate Their Own Omnipotence

Hah! And we look on grandly, look
at the poor souls labyrinthed in minds
that look upon us grandly, make
schemes to fit us into their schemes.

We know better. We know that spooks
like us are figments, that the mind
creates, inflates, destroys, then fakes
its own death. Things are as they seem

for those with clipboards, dignitaries
in long white coats, sad-eyed, who've felt
escape escape them. Tired, dotty,
they fumble and squint and assume

they are alive, while in our room:
skeleton escapes from body,
marrow escapes from bone and melts
away in silent tributaries.

In the Train Station Watching Footage
of a Plane Striking a Building

O mankind! We created you from a single pair of man and woman,
and made you into nations and tribes, that ye may know each other...
—al-Qur'an 49:13

And so it is that certain tragedies
seem to float across the sky
at arbitrary points in our field of vision:
the smoking shells of buildings, colorless
streams of gas hissing from overturned tractor-trailers,
rail cars crinkled amidst clumps of oak and pine;
our own small horrors trail off them like tow ropes,
wind-whipped cords braided from pink slips,
falls from trees, a split lip beneath the jungle gym,
this or that parent embalmed and sleeping...
in the great spaces between each lies cancer, idolatry
and the instinct for joy that struggles to float free
from the mind and the eyes that fail to see.
Such tragedies are crumbs left on the trail
and the crows, the crows are everywhere...

I stand and watch commuters huddle
along the platform, watch
them board their trains, uncertain, afraid
of becoming part of an unwanted history,
a story of Empires: seep
and contract, cleave asunder
and coalesce: I watch as we gather
like rainwater pooling on a ledge.
How do we persist, with so much
to despise, so much to withhold, such a constant
baring of teeth, it is remarkable
we have not devoured ourselves completely...

And instead, on the day a far off speck
grew immense and black in the sky,

on a day when our magistrate slunk fearfully

from trench to trench, a day that saw an island smoke,
when the dead in their numbers crowded the turnstiles
and the next world shuddered from the weight of them
and the shudder was felt here, in our teeth, we turned
to one another and with a glance, apologized
for every wrong we had done, and all those
we'd imagined done to us. What we found, on such a day,
reminds us we are human,
and it leers at us from the blind heart of the forest,
and it waits with the patience of a seed,
and it thrives on tears as well as rainwater.

The cat has gone missing

What can have happened,
what grave concern has called to her,
has extracted her from the places I make comfortable:
pillows, paper bags, the spot by the stove
where she suffers poorly chosen food...
all those things
she will miss, or not, she's gone.

By the time it was one hundred thousand
years ago we'd made it to logos, ritualized
cannibalism, learned to chip tools,
but it took another ninety six
thousand before we could domesticate the cat.
Four thousand years alongside humans
and still she goes, when the wind tells her,
away to die. Others, people mostly,
need to be told when, and where, and even why,
all those answers
we crave, or not, and are gone. Cats just go.

Revisiting a Theme

A fat grey squirrel waddles at winter's edge,
over a curb, past an abandoned tire.
Crooked homes tilt toward the sidewalk,
draw forth a scene buried deep in the synapses:
there, on that street, age four, my pants fell to my ankles
first time I tried to rollerskate.
I screamed for help and no one came.
Perhaps the fat grey squirrel's great-
great-great-great-grandfather watched
as my sobs ceased, as I figured out
how to untie, to untangle, to unbind and walk away.

Waltzing Toward Slumber

It's not a beautiful thing, not really;
it's just the way the evening light
sliced up by the structure's unwalled frame
signals the end of a day's work;
and how follows an *adiós,*
hasta mañana to the crew, and finally
the long, liquid drive back home.
Or how tonight
you have set out candles
and made a special dinner,
or perhaps your boss
has given you hell again so we vent
and munch crackers,
then go out and drink too much
      and maybe sing
and probably cry.
Or else your latest test results
peeking out from their envelope
mean our hill is growing steeper,
and so begins another night
of soft, rare whispers,
the invocation of future memory,
warmth mingling until sleep overcomes us on the couch.
It's not beautiful, but it is all we will ever have;
how the tears and the gentle hand
pouring the wine
etch the same lines in time,
the scratching of your chest
along my back; because at the end
of each day's work is you, and at the end of you
is twilight, and then another day, and then perhaps another.

Shepherd at Pause in the Rain-Shadow

But then of course no one knows
if we live now, or in some paradise
perpetually henceforth,
nor if some black-fanged beast waits,
lounging on its soft haunches;
but I have my small idea
of love-in-the-world,
and it obeys me
the way a cloud
obeys the logic of clouds.

Following Ghosts Upriver

originally published in 2010 by Main St. Rag Publishing

Following Ghosts Upriver, 1

part one

All these sad, broken towns
strewn with rusted oil drums
and pallets, stacked and rotting,
are my home, every one.
Along the Mohawk, the Niagara,
the oily Genesee,
run the tracks and the trains
and the passengers on their way
somewhere bright, somewhere
with a hint of glamour, somewhere
not like the dead little towns
they have left behind. I was born
under their rooflines, drank
from their sooty wells,
learned that their borders,
stubbled with briar,
were the edges of love; that grace
was a crumpled cardboard box
thrusting a flap skyward
from the sidewalk; and that
the evening fire beckoned to us
from the hearth
because it was dying.
Watching the streets and the spaces
between them blur by, I know
I have been away too long in places bright
and not so glamorous,
but not so long, a voice humming up
from the engine tells me,
that I have forgotten
how to peel off my shoes
and pull a chair up beside the embers
and start to place my small sticks,
one by one, upon the coals.

Desire Algebraic

First, an aunt, half-asleep after third shift,
drifted across the median
into a school bus. Witness: the crumpled hood
of her just-paid for car, the closed casket,
and the consistency of this closing act
with the rest of her days: no one else
was injured. Weeks later, an old man,
her father, farm-raised and all his life
a prodigious spreader of seed, at last
had enough of his body withering, shrinking
in knobs and folds, so he turned into chaff
and blew away.

After the second funeral, the ghost of Pythagoras
came whispering through the pews: *who,*
who will be the third?
Two is divisible, weak and composed
of lonely symmetries, of ones forced together
so obviously... but three, the triangular,
lends an extra dimension, one that seems
a source of wisdom, and nothing
adds dimension to a coordinate plane
like death—there must be a third,
we cannot make meaning without
proper sacrifice, the latch drawn shut,
the smell of blood, of life underground.

Of course there were no volunteers; instead,
we all took hysterical care while driving,
walking, noticing gratefully
that the Government Building
had no thirteenth floor. Instead, tonight
we are mathematicians
all, seers waiting for the surge

of wisdom that will come
when the formula is complete,
when three emerges from the collapse of two
and one from naught,
from tziphra, sipos, tsiphron, rota,
circulus, galgal, theca, null, sunya, as-sifr--
from the only number, beneath which
all the others go, the brilliant O, figura nihili.

Good Friday

1.
Kneeling in the hayloft, she prays
in winter light. The new calf's bleating
quiets in the stall beneath,
the mother's shuffling hooves, snorts,
all falls a hush. The light prickles
against her eyelids, she prays
into a beam of yellowed heat
that blocks off the path to God:

Gloria in excelsis deo,
et in terra pax hominibus bonae voluntatis
Laudamus te.
Benedicimus te. I cannot see you
O Lord, I cannot hear your voice.
I look in the sun for you
and cannot find you, I search
the skies and fields and the eyes
of my children and cannot
find you. Adoramus te.
Glorificamus te.

Every morning, she breaks a loaf
into six pieces, makes six bundles,
each with perhaps an egg, a piece
of boiled beef, a rind of cheese,
snug beside the bread. Every morning
she sends her husband off to the fields,
theirs' or the landlords'; the older
sons will join him in another year.
And every morning, chores finished,
the children go in a knot up the road
to school, books and bundles astride them.
Only then, once they have gone
over the rise, once her own early chores

are finished, does she climb the hayloft
and pray until her crooked body sways
to the sound of another voice,
and she prays harder, and begs for help,
and no help comes, and she fights
the devil until the corn sheller calls,
until the loom shuttle calls, until
the new calf starts to moan and the chickens
scream from across the yard
at the devil taking flight and his shadow
passing over them.

2.
Her husband worries and is kind,
brings her a book of paper to write in,
a new rosary, fine boots worth more
than they can afford. She fills the boots
with manure and eggshells,
hides the rosary in a coffee can,
opens the book in a rage
and digs the nib into it, the word
is God and God is the word,
black ink squelching the white fire
of the pages.

Lord, I cannot find you,
the Devil has hid you behind the sun,
the world is too bright and I cannot
find you. Gratias agimus tibi propter
magnam gloriam tuam.
Domine Deus, Rex caelestis, Deus Pater omnipotens.
Domine fili unigenite, Jesu Christe.
Save me Lord and I will give you
everything, all that I am all
that I have…

The children look side-eyed
when she dyes all their clothes purple,

underclothes, coats, mittens. The better
to hide in from the Devil's light,
she thinks, watching her husband trudge
off to town to fetch the doctor.

3.
Molly and I found her journal
at a flea market upstate, wedged
between junior league cookbooks.
We sat in the motel and watched
her script grow smaller and smaller,
her prayers reverse light and dark,
her last oath to God and then pages
of black on black, ink scribbled
into dense and moonless thatch.

We read about how the doctor came
and brought her things to drink,
but his potions were of the Devil,
and she poured them on the ground
where they hissed and smoked. We saw
her husband's eyes begin to shine
with the Devil's light, how she crept
up on him with a poker, red from the fire,
how he woke and knocked her down. She
made her final oath, the pages
went black, and she ran out to the barn
to sway there in the quiet dark,
free from the Devil and the blinding light:
Domine Deus, Agnus Dei, Filius patris.
Qui tollis peccata mundi, miserere nobis.
Qui tollis peccata mundi suscipe deprecationem nostram.
Qui sedes ad dexteram patris miserere nobis.
Quoniam tu solus sanctus.
Tu solus Dominus.
Tu solus Altissimus, Jesu Christe.
Cum Sancto Spiritu in gloria Dei Patris. Amen.

Easter two days off, she brushes
the hay from her knees, descends
full of the Lord's light. Her husband is lit
with Devil's flame and yells,
breath reeking of the underworld.
He cannot touch her.
The stairs do not squeak underfoot,
the door swings open before her
though she puts no hand upon it.
She stands in the children's room
and bathes them in the Lord's light.
I will keep my promise.

Tucked in behind the last few pages
a clipped obituary, the youngest boy
who fell from a window Good Friday's
eve and broke his neck. The last legible
page of block letters: MY SON FELL
AND I CULD NOT CATCH HIM.
When Molly closed the book
and sipped from her plastic cup,
I could tell she was staring
at a place out beyond our time together,
past our half-hearted fights and worn-thin
love. I could tell by the way she smiled
as though it was the first time she'd ever seen me.

Animal Logic and the Hub

The flight to Pittsburgh was oversold
and a voice on the loudspeaker
    begged for volunteers,
for the flexibly scheduled, for *heroes*:
this is how we live. We walk the gangplank
    to a winged metal tube
and are flung to distant cities,
we disembark and wonder at the mess
we've made of our children,
    our parents, our homes,
our gods, our health;
we make do and cringe at the presence
    of other people, we preen
and draw them toward us,
we puff up our chests and laugh
    too loudly, we recoil
when another claims us
as part of some not-so-royal "we."

As it is and always has been,
but further bent into our selves,
as it is and will someday cease to be,
bundles of nerve and blood embroidered
with the sound of pictures, the color
of word, each of us ready, at an instant,
to don the cape and pose on a mound of dead--
to be heroes, and not to fly.

How I Almost Nodded Off
(or, I imagine a baby rat in my mouth
as I wait for my beloved to come home)

Ah! I hear the screen door slap shut,
    feet clogging down the hallway,
        and then a tap-tap-tapping coming from behind one
            front tooth, my tooth:

these are the sounds my head snaps awake too, the sounds
of a collapsing rhythm (sleep), sounds (sleep)
    that celebrate their (sleep) demise themselves, old and dying gods
snuggling up for a last mug of ichor,
sounds lodged in the cracks

of the day-to-day, of our monument thereof,

    the bold, stern faces we war with
        and take charge with and make good time with
        and fuck with, if it's like that,

        build stone faces with, riddled with sparrow-holes,
            with the nests of smaller mites,
                single-celled colonies alive
                      in the soft folds
                          around the eyes—

like the faces alive on my favorite t-shirt, the
red one, torn and threadbare,
    (it mocked the gods of easter island, they
        unlikely to sue for libel)
a stony but slightly animate face, one eyebrow raised
    as though it heard feet coming down the hallway
    (jackbooted feet? No, they're cleverer now,
    feet in soft-soled italian loafers,
    feet clattering in wooden Buddha sandals).

That shirt, my shirt, an expression of perfect paranoia and now stolen,
    stolen by some or another rag-dreamer,
    made into a flag, or—no, now I remember,
        I cast it into the trash in a fit, a fit that demanded:
all outerwear
invested with memory must
        to the discard pile go. (they were creepy, the judge
            and jury and all the rest of the crew that built
            the decree,
    but then I was creepy too, fair bet).

O man, I got that shirt at the state fair, with my moms, no, I
got it at the MOMA Koons exhibit, with Auntie Bedelia, no,
    well, whatever, wherever, I liked that shirt
    but that was a long time ago, I was on a fixed income
        and I moved on, off into the redwoods for a bit
            then to the city of slaughterhouses.

No more budgets now, I go for splurging, now, wastefulness—mindful wasting!
    Dragging the earth and all her people down with me.
There are, to wit, wieners presently on the grill,

    wieners roasting within their various names, spitting little seeds of hot fat
on the coals; wieners are meant to hiss and sizzle, to speak,
    they say: Robert Vaughn! Robert Vaughn! And what could it mean
        but there is Robert Vaughn on the back porch,
            on the table, on a kitchen magnet sent
from Gary Myers, attorney-at-law, willing to take my case.

See Robert Vaughn's head leap from the table to my eye!
See how stern his stony face, see how it explodes
into my eye! He was an actor, he played a spy and blah blah blah

    and now his stern stony face is a value-added object

that pops! Explodes into the sleepy matrices
    of my recognition! Robert Vaughn,
        on a kitchen magnet, on the small green plastic

              patio table
              that sits on my back porch
                  beside an empty Tidy Cats Multi-Cat litter carton
    and the overflowing recycleable bin.
And omigod there really are—mastodonic, furious—footsteps

    coming down the hallway: pull
    the covers to the chin, there are no covers,
    only wieners and a steaming back porch
    and the end of summer, instead: must
                      visualize
        mommy…

    and omigod, turns out it's love making all that racket,
    witless and strong as a dying animal,
    gnaw-your-own-foot-off love,
  my daily habit and all the daily re-enactments
of my daily habit: love-as-it-is, love in the world,
you as the locus of my heart emerging,
    you as the locus of a landscape suddenly gorged with love,
        you as the altar,
                I as the pew, the prayer rug,
                      the bent knee, the folded hand,
                          the eye in perfect focus.
And this is what I fear and celebrate as fear?
These are the sounds turn a face from stone to flesh?

    No more monuments, not stone, not flesh, they make us pigeons,
    they make us slide around in the foam and shit
    trying to draw a bead on glory like it was a life raft
    and not a bag of rocks,
    trying even to harvest the Killer from fields of children,
        to trim the Stoolie from yards of scripture,
                to extract god from the light and the light
    from the ever-popular Waking Moment,
all for a bag of rocks…

    but never mind, where is my shirt? And the tapping behind

my tooth, my tongue hides in the back of my mouth,
      hides from the rat that tries endlessly to dig its way out,
  never succeeds,
whines like a broken fanbelt day in, day out...
     I suppose it's only the nature of rats to try
  and escape,
            and the tap-tap-tapping behind my front tooth
              that just won't quit.
is only a rat psalm, a way to escape by celebrating
  our inability to escape,

And then the door opens and you smile and my rat sprouts wings--

Executive Privilege

He put his hand in her face
and fumbled with the baffles;
Pretty kitty, pretty kitty,
and an expensive cat at that,
he fumbled with the baffles
until something wrong went "snap"
and kitty slumped.

In line at the business center
pretty kitty in a box
beneath his arm: no surprise
how that turned out, no refund
no return, tech support =
2 pints of plasma/hour.

And he needs his blood to eat,
and his clones all failed
in the summer heat,
his credit stamp a faded smear,
pretty kitty won't get fixed
this year or any year, the way
his luck's been going.

But the office must count
for something, as patriots insist,
and so he broadcasts his plea
on the afternoon feed:

Your President needs your help,
dignity, other heads of state,
Pretty Kitty! Please vote today.

They watch the numbers tick by,
pretty kitty a sack of wires,

Mr. President a sad old man--
sad enough for the referendum
to pass. Tech support, orange suits,
a blur in the oval office:
pretty kitty purrs at last.

Research and Development

Farinelli saw the stars land
and he sang to them his castrati
and the stars turned and ran
back across the filament
and up into their spheres.

Two is the number of countesses
suicided after I was Adelaide,
one is the number of digits
I gave freely, and would give again,
and naught the number of rude butchers,
maids, farmers, paint-mixers, and dogs
*who've ever **run** from my bejeweled voice.*
Thus puzzled, he pressed his head
to a perfumed pillow and slept.

He did not wake when the stars
returned, silent as death;
did not stir as they hovered about him,
thinking at one another;
only dreamed gently as they departed
once again, unable to conceive
a means to strap and mount his voice
beside the pulse cannon at the prow
of their battle cruiser.

Mirabilia

Mid-morning rain indulges us a pattern
even as it vexes us our parades and al fresco,
hurtling down from the substantial nowhere
we often glimpse when in planes,
wedged in too-narrow seats,
peeking out the too-small windows
at the space between clouds. We have glass-bottomed
boats, and should build jetliners
the same way; Wonder Woman
had a transparent plane,
after all, though explaining
this concept to, say, Roger Bacon
might prove difficult, some rainy mid-morning
in a nook amongst the dreaming spires,
over mead and a table scattered
with lenses and vellum…
better to just buy him a ticket on the Concorde
and a knapsack full of comic books
then meet him at JFK
with a strong cup of coffee
and some Lebanese hash.
He's going to need both, as will you,
before the two of you start working
on nature's veil again, and even if you
are not, and plan instead to spend the evening
lost in the tortured lights of Times Square.

part two
Following Ghosts Upriver, 2

Grinding up through the Cumberland gap
in a rented panel truck
stuffed with boxes of wine and oil,
umbrellas, socks, all the detritus
plucked and condensed from
the Kuiper belt of objects
drawn into orbit by the force of our habits
and our habits' habits;
grinding up from Atlanta
and its nest in the piedmont,
from a New City full of nothing
but a surging tide of options
and derivatives, upon which floats
all the usual trophies desired
by souls who believe money
the fruit of all good. Atlanta is no
sprinting maiden stopping
for golden apples, nor is Hippomenes'
golden youth alive in the sun;
no, it is there, in the stall
at the edge of the crowd,
the one selling souvenir fruit
painted gold, and silver too—
that is where Atalanta lives,
and she carries water and food
in to the merchant, suffers his rapes
and belt, dreams of killing him,
taking over the stall, bronzing his organs
and placing them among the wares…

And so we grind up out of her lap,
over the piedmont, through the gap
into Tennessee, the same verdant, endless
ripple of ridges dusty, pocked soldiers

once stumbled home over,
bred between, built clapboard churches
and radio towers upon,
learned to sell fireworks and horses along...
the truck rocks and strains going up,
rocks and hums going down,
lulls us both but we are together
in America and so each take turns
jarring the other awake. On the plateau
we nod at horses dappling the late
afternoon fields, listen
to preachers shouting about God
and Liberals, about Just Rewards
and Welfare Queens, about the many
Righteous Wars they believe themselves
to be fighting. Night is sudden,
or we missed the last light wink off,
and the trucks take over, headlights
meld into serpents, erupt from
behind crests ahead, blast the interior
of the truck cab and drag boxy shadows
along your sleeping face. Alone

in America, on our way home, Kentucky
and Ohio and Pennsylvania
announcing themselves
from the shoulder, spreading varieties
of highway greenery and cardboard hotels
before us, we have only to stop
and stretch out beside
a gas pump, watch aging motorcyclists
adjust their pants, offer
money to the young cashier, her face
a coiled snake ready to strike,
to understand: we are not alone
in America, or anywhere else;
we are not even ourselves,
but then we get back in the truck

and begin to move again
along the road, to forget
that you and I are fictions,
and then faith creeps in like mold
and the stories start to tell themselves,
and we are: almost there,
hoping we have left behind
Atlanta, the piedmont, all the things
we once drove toward.
     The child
cries out in the night not
to see if his mother still exists
but to remind himself that he does;
so it is with the highways
of America, each car a cozy bed
sliding over monsters too slow
to catch us, every mile
another cry meant to dispel
the blind and murderous night.

There's Never a Line

In a desperate little restaurant
filled with small-town lawyers
and legislators, fat and rosy,
where the table sags and we sag
with it, where the waitress tries
to keep from crying, we
smile and pile our dishes for her,
we brush crumbs from the table
and rub our bellies happily,
but not too happily, though the meal
was made from blood and song.

Eyes and the top of a head appear
in the window of the swinging door,
peep you, and disappear; you tell me
we're being watched, and I say yes,
I know, we are the guts of a lamb,
the paths of doves flung into the sky,
the cracks splintering an oracle bone.
The eyes, the waitress, the fearful
men in shopworn suits, all are trying
to read us: are they
wealthy investors? Hired killers?
Merely lost? And there is no way
for us to reply: no, we live here now,
we are like you, hidden chef,
sad-eyed server, small-time
power-monger.

There is no way because
we are not like them yet,
we have too many things to forget,
too many new steps to learn
before we find ourselves

peeking out at the new faces, trying
to draw strength and some future tense
from the curve of an unfamiliar neck,
the set of the shoulders, from the way
they wipe their mouths, then recede
back into the loam of somewhere else.

At The Niagara County Landfill and Recycling Center
(or, The Believer Among Us)

Seraphim, cherubim, from cut earth they rise,
from pipes bent like hooks, emerging, they rise,
ophanim glaze upwards, the muddy sky
shimmers, the air bent with angels
who sing as they rise.

At his throne
Stavros sits, from his throne calls down judgment
on the truck that now idles, now straddles the scale.
The weights are recorded, the angels are witness,
malakhim, hashmallim, they watch from above,
over mud the wheels go, elohim, they roll,
and Stavros is left to watch the air glow.

With black fire he numbers, on white fire
records them, while archangels whisper
the trisagion: *Agios o Theos, agios ischyros,*
agios athanatos, eleison imas.
From the throats of the angels,
as the grumbling trucks pass,
the song quakes through Stavros
like garbage to gas.

Economic Development Seminar

The blast furnace quakes to life, the girders
spidered up around it
shudder in sympathy, then the rivets start
to keen... it's been dead thirty months,
the tower and conveyor, the furnace dome,
the skimmer; thirty months
since slag oozed out, thirty months since any pig iron
squealed free from a chunk of hematite.

Fall has daubed the world from the edges inward
    with mud and honey and ash
and ghosts swing from the porches and wait
    for the mendicants to come,
begging sweets. A hole in the chain link fence
    bordering veteran's park
grants egress to teens and vagrants,
    spills them out onto the railroad tracks
and the rusted boxcars strewn
    like pieces of type on a printer's floor.

Most nights, when they meet
on the path--the teens gangling free
from their falling houses
and the rooted hobos who dig loaves
from dumpsters--they glance
side-eyed across time at each other, giggle,
mutter, move on, but tonight, with the smell
    of burning coke and limestone
tinting the air, the young ones offer
    skittish hellos, the old men grimace
and hand them bottles of wine,
    and they stand together for a moment
watching the flames lick at the stars.

The Grinding Wears the Stone Down, Too

These were the days of the week: 6 am: rise, evacuate, preen,
mumble at the pigeons on the ledge.
Morning light hissing up from the underworld
as I made toast. Butter for you, jelly for me,
7 am: kiss-and-part, ache, endure,
then home again and, perhaps, the weight of you.

      And thus I became a cretin,
fat
and grateful
for every little jelly stain
and buttery lip. Home by 6 most days of the week,
weekends a fog of crumpled sheets
and tree-lined strolls; these were the scenes that dug
a hole in my skull, trepanned me
and let all the wrong of this world leak out.
Specific details are nothing, they make you a fool,
a town idiot fumbling with beads and string—
they will make you a believer,
      and that should be warning enough.

Use my example, tack my photo
to kindergarten walls: this is what happens when you believe
that details add up to something more
than another detail, this is what happens
when 5 pm comes, when the train shudders into the station,
your hands stained, your ears full of chatter, your dank stairs,
your oven lit, your glass of vodka, the stupid way you sit
and wait. Wait to hear a key
squeak the lock. To feel a hand
upon your neck. For all details
to fade into mush, for the truck
to come and haul away her clothes,
for the lake to swallow her ashes

and turn them into fish. This is what belief
gets you, children: half a man,
surrounded by details,
waiting to be rid of them and all that they insinuate.

Ice Sculpture

The bus chugs on between mounds of snow.
She watches it go, then tugs open her scarf
to let the cold start to kiss her throat;
at home, she'll prop the window up and let
the clean night air come stroke her 'till she floats
away, to become the beat of her heart
slowed, her body at rest, free from knowledge.

The dogs who live next door whine and wake her;
a door opens, they tumble down the stairs
and bark and bounce and shit. She grits her teeth,
then to herself recites her morning prayer:
"I swear upon my mother's grave, I'll kill
those dogs one day." She hears them tumble back
upstairs, hears the owner coo, smells an egg
start to fry, and tries to stay perfectly still.

In Praise of Winter

A circle of leaves the color
    of just-ripe lemons
glows in the the yard, a sky as gray
    and pocked as concrete
seethes above them; no, the world
is not upside down: it's early November
    in Western New York, go,
stuff the chinks with paper, go,
split your logs and clean the radiators.

Murder will wait 'till March, or April; now
    is the time of bells
waiting to be struck. Incurious sapling
teens rush and twitter along the sidewalk
    homeward to their video clusters,
incurious pulpy adults appear
    and blow lemony leaves
down and over the curb; everyone
cannot stand still and everyone
walks slightly hunched, cowering, dogs
    sensing a raised hand.
The bell will soon sound, the earth
    will vanish
and whiten and grow slick.
I keep my heathen prayers to myself:
I can scarcely wait to taste the first flakes,
to feel the first uncontrollable shudder,
the wind that turns my bones to glass.

Squirrels fat as bankers stop to watch
    my small dance, my snow
prayer: head cocked, peering at the sky,
a coarse wind shears up over the escarpment
and blows the folds of my coat open.

    I pull it back against my waist
and laugh. Five months of dark, cold,
    and sleet, a tunnel stretching
from autumnal wealth to the first
nude shoots of spring. There is a snarl
    of wires in my brain
and it blinks out a code, the story
written on the walls of the dome
it grew beneath: ice, thaw, burn, harvest,
    then prepare for ice again.

I keep my heathen prayers to myself,
white-lipped, quivering, waiting for the song
of snow, the deathless wind
that mocks the embers
even as it teases them back to flame.

part three
Stare Decesis

Doves in fist, campfire visible from the valley,
we settled down among the lemon trees.
We sat and bled the doves beside the fire and ate.

Every third Saturday the pastor came and slept,
and three times a year we visited him,
and once a year we did nothing all day long.

We tried to love one another because we snap like dolls,
and when we went up into the mountains, looking
for doves, we sang about the trees burning down.

Once upon a time I heard a song of riches,
endless doves perched on cedar limbs.
but then again, once upon a time, I was a child.

Carnivalesque

In every town lives the woman who never bathes
and talks into a dead cell phone she pulled from a dumpster,
and in every town lives the man whose face
sprouts new sores daily, whose nose holds broken glasses
five times too large
suspended over stolen false teeth
three times too small.
Every town has them, but ours are in charge.

Hence, the street lights burn a pale green,
hence the bell tower is slanted
and the bell stuffed with dead gulls.
The alleyways and rooflines
burn words of fire into the skull,
and the keys to the city are given to anyone who asks,
      though the keyhole has great rusty fangs.

The voice in the dead cell phone tells her to walk
and we have a parade; his false teeth fall
into the canal and we hold our annual fishing derby.
You probably don't understand,
      if you're not from around here,
why we like things the way they are,
and the only way really to explain it
is to ask what other places are like
and then shake our heads, ashamed
at such atrocities, such savagery,
astounded at how a soul must suffer
when trapped in tidy lands, ruled by wise old kings.

The Flare

When the bird came down the chimney
And shrieked over the dinner table
Into the den, father chased after
With a blanket, and we trailed behind
Like kites. Trapped under a wool
Coverlet printed with green trout,
The bird beat its wings, leapt
And thrashed, made a muffled noise
Like a heart gone mad, even as father
scooped and gathered the ends
of the blanket in his hands.

Out in the snow, flung from
The blanket, the bird lay still and twitched
One wing. *Is it broken?* As we fell
To whispering, no one saw
It fly away, but all at once the little hole
In the snow was empty save for
A few brown feathers. Walking

From the barn, thirty-five years later,
I saw a hole with exactly the same
Shape and color and feathery
Texture, but forming out
On the horizon, immense,
Hovering, across a snowy field of stubble.
All at once I felt something beat
Its wings inside my chest, felt it leap
And thrash; before I could
Spill it out onto the snow, something else
Awoke, beneath my feet and the earth
And beneath space and it rose up
To the flutter in my chest
and consumed it in a burst of light.

The flare has stayed in my skull

Like the ghost of a flash bulb
For months, dim and lurking
In a corner while I cut hay or watch
The new foal wobble about,
But it brightens as if to blind me
When I forget, and start to think
About mexicans taking all the jobs
Or how stupid my children are
Or how glad I am the wife died
When she did. It must be cells
Gone crazy in my brain, tumors
On top of tumors. Time is short.
Yesterday I stood, staring

At my car keys in a parking lot
Like the story of the universe
Was written in their grooves,
The way they suck light in,
Spit it back out again, the shadow
And filigree and brassy glare
Played their music on my eyes
Until I cried for the thirteenth time
That day, at nine o-clock in the morning.

Strategy and Tactics

The cat's head swelled and grew transparent
'till it filled the room, the sound of breathing
and little pips of synapse floating over my bed.
I could not raise an arm to wipe it away,
to thrash and tear the wispy skull;
when she began to purr, black water came
and swallowed me.
              When I woke,
she was gone, off cleaning herself
or reporting to central cat command the results
of the latest experiment, how quickly
the drugs secreted in my kielbasa
had taken effect.
    I am a willing subject, of course,
since I love her so and the way she shapes
my life. I scoop her shit from a box
and make it clean for her, I rub her
until she swipes at me and lays long red
tracks on my arm. Many's the worse arrow
I've suffered in exchange for love
and companionship; if I must be a cog
in the ongoing feline occupation, so be it.

Other forces are at play, as well; why not
throw my lot in with the kitties?
When the television clicks on in the dark
and hard, fractal faces begin to spiral
in and out of themselves, laughing and calling
my dead soul to puppet life, I bear them
but offer no love, I swear to do
              what they ask
and I lie, go on about the business of living,
such as it is. I would throw my lot
in with the kitties and must, soon,

because I cannot lie forever, they will know,
they are probably reading this now,
over my shoulder, planning the height
of the judge's chair, rising the blood fever
of the jury, polishing the manacles
in anticipation of the next moonless night.

Lunar Spring Thaw

Across the street a little girl screams
the way only children can: a scream
of delight, but still, every grown-up
in every yard turns their head to check.

She is taunting gravity with a puddle,
splashing banana-yellow boots down
into the muddy meltwater, drops
arcing out into space or bending back
to speckle the hem of her pink coat
and her improbably white leggings,
even up to the gleaming red coil
of her face.

She screams again when her mother
backhands her cheek, doubles its color,
and then once more as she is yanked
by the arm up to the house. More heads turn,
tsk, tsk, turn away. Above them, the moon
just now clearing the roofline is pocked
and scarred wherever bits of dust and rock
and ice have struck her, because the moon
has no atmosphere, all her scars come
in silence. Here on earth, scars
come silent and deafening and all
frequencies between, and so
we who are mostly water
must learn to build, layer by layer,
our own atmospheres, stripes of
troposphere, stratosphere, mesosphere,
sheathing to deflect
the smallest bolides and break
larger ones into fragments that flame

the night sky, so we might
make wishes at them.

But some among us never learn the trick
and instead remain as moons, noiseless
and present, craters and pocks aglow
for all to see, waxing and waning,
tugging the oceans of human love
to and fro. This night, the moon seems
to take up the whole of the sky, lighting
the street bone-blue; in such light
the girl's mother comes out to the street
again, screaming herself now, into a cell phone.
In the upstairs window a small face, freshly
scrubbed, ashen, watching her mother's body
bend and twitch and dream of velocity.

House and Door and Window

Becalmed in the moment after a fight
my wife and I retreat to our respective
corners and listen to the washing machine
as it creaks and thuds, its belt worn,
its drum running crooked; it creaks
and thuds and then hits a new cycle,
one that makes a noise like the slow,
ponderous flapping wings of a bird
the size of a jetliner, the very one
now interposing itself between my eyes
and the squared sunlight, soaking it up
until I can no longer see her, or
myself.
    So I fumble about, blind and waving
my hands in little half-circles until they hit
something solid, something wooden
and cold, and I turn it over with my fingers
and then walk on, still holding the thing,
praying silently that I have not left
the cellar door open.

Sonnets Are Stupid

Everyone looks stupid when they run,
even the graceful and swift: the cheetah
looks stupid, a clump of meat and muscle
and nail and tooth, stupidly angling

toward an ibix, too stupid to starve.
And everyone looks stupid while they fuck,
though not many of us care, or we care
because we are taking stupid aim at

babymaking, a whole stupid family tree:
*"Certain stupid creatures, walking upright,
can shape the steam rising from their heads
into phonetic clusters: air? stone? fire?
gravity? the red moon? Stupid titles
given to the galaxies astride them."*

Thank You For Showing Me The Way Home

--for Ashley

There's this man, and he's telling us about
another man whose memory was blasted
apart, every six seconds he restarts, the world
is new and it's 1956, because it started then,
his endless loop.

The story sets me sprawling along
fevered byways, neuronal speculative
storms, impossible things, like:

      how could it ever
come to pass
that I no longer recognize
your face, in summer slanted light,
whispering to me, smiling softly?
My own brain is already damaged enough
from love that I cannot even think it,
I may as well fail to recognize my own
body surrounding me.

      And so, because it may, in fact,
come to pass that my brain is blasted
and left in less exotic shreds, I've come
      to offer you
these words--not much, I know,
but that's what I have to give, and before you
      were my life I had
not even such a little thing
as a poem
of love.

The Frequency is in the Upper Reaches of the Band

That is, the frequency with which I take water up to the fire god,
the god that rides me when I am on fire
and alone. Ha, a brave way to put it, "fire god,"
a brave name he's given him, brave for the patron
of self-love. The frequency with which
I take water to him is alarming to both of us,
but both profit: I am ridden and made
to pull at the bit, he gets steam. To be ridden
breaks the loneliness up into bytes and pixels,
and I have no idea what he does with the steam.
A fair trade. Our chins wiggle, we slink away afterward
like opposing lawyers who've just shared a foul joke
about the afternoon judge.

Love is hemorrhaging out of where the scab used to be,
I can feel the wet running slowly along my skin,
pushing down small hairs like lava over pine
and I like it, I am a factory of love and you,
my precious, provide me planks and ores and electricity
enough for a nation meant to infect all the globe
with color. And yet you are away, our suppliers are turning
their work over to shadowy sub-contractors: world
domination will have to wait, and so
the frequency with which I slip a nail
under the scab and pry it up is alarming, I like it.
I like it and carry water up the little knoll and drown
the little god over and over again; only such discipline
assures that I do not drown you,
when you return, in love, in blood, in fire, in steam, in all of it.

Following Ghosts Upriver, part 3

A fat belly in your 40's makes rise
the risk of dementia, of statistics
proving the knoll we cannot see around
is really there, or at least some angle
of descent, some topographical tic,
is quantifiable, it cannot be
that the science we make things alive with
is so frail, we must believe it, we must,

but not to the point of action, of course,
though my fat belly is nearly 40,
and I did climb the stairs repeatedly
today, if only to move dull green boxes
overfilled with Christmas sparkles and bulbs
up to the third floor. Wasn't belly-fear
made me climb, although belly-fear's the source
of not a few inglorious moments
in my life, and I'm not sure dementia
didn't reach me some time ago. Oh well,

another one for the newspaper pile
that teeters on the dog food bin, threatens
to turn our kitchen into Manila;
maybe some day we'll live on it, squatting
in the refuse while columnists
argue the use-value of our labor.
Or else our fat bellies will drive us mad,
mad and trapped in swells of snow shoulder-high,
not even some rich man's trash heap to feed on.

That's how things are up near the cataract,
up near where the Niagara trips over rock
and out further too, where wrinkled fields

hang between lake and river, the escarpment
run through the middle like a washing line.

It is hard here, but not dire; our dump
remains buried, farms abound and flourish;
we have, in other words, an excellent
view of America's descent into
sludge and grime. Think of it as a kind of

water-park ride, where at the end you must
suffocate in bad debt and discarded
tires. Not so bad, much better than most,
livable enough to write poems, sure. Example:
walking home after too much whiskey
I met a boy with a mouth full of spit
and a brain muddled by constant want;
I gave him my change and told him not to join
the army; war is mean and a bad virus to catch
but anyway, I just knew they'd never have him,
I hoped to save him one more indignity
piling on. Weeks later I saw his picture

in the local paper, arrested for molesting
an 11-year old girl. Maybe the army was not
such a bad idea after all. This is where we live,
America falling over rocks, in slow motion,
and no amount of threats to my 40-year old belly
is going to stop me from pouring a few more
glasses into it, not while I've reason enough
and time and the moon overhead and love
everywhere, not while such evidence
remains hidden to goddamn nearly everyone.

Little City Breakdown

Animals taught us to be in the world,
and we abused the lesson

not in our murdering, but in killing
without sacrifice. For example: the city council meeting:
    monkey-brained bureaucrats

clawing each other to death
on a low stage, shooting slides

writ with rules of jurisprudence
onto a white canvas screen,--

a hundred sets of teeth grinding,
    the sound of skinks snapped in two by the pump-shed hinge:--

mutation or virus, whatever it was
made us so wordy and dense,
made us lose track of those we've killed,

may be only the echo of myself lashing myself together

from scraps of all the stories I've heard.
All of them. But because I am an echo
I might be the real thing, and the virus or mutation
makes me say fuck it anyway, who cares when
a pot of basil growing please me and the spot on your
    neck where the hairs stand up please me and the
nasty look I get from everyone sometimes please me
and the sound of goats please me and all
        the baseball cards I stole and then lost please me
    and offering the whole archipelago to the enemy please me and god in
his monkey-day tweeds please me and we took the day together to walk in
the autumn light and hold one another, and that, that is all there is...

and once it has pleased me, and then,
and then all the cars shrunk into the void
and all the car stereos shrunk into the void
and all the fire hydrants shrunk into the void
and all the ice cream shrunk into the void
and all the birch trees shrunk into the void
and all the flavored lozenges
and all the magma that all of it sat on shrunk into the void
and all the world thus shrunk into the void
and I was pleased, and you were pleased,
and you are the one I remember
and lie with
and live with and then I can hear the

---terror systems alert---

insects, clouds of them,
just outside the window. The cat's paw
beneath the door, pink and grasping,
the pulpy hot tang of fresh chlorine
from the neighbor's pool.

An infinity of compassion spurts across the universe
like ink on silk, sliding, settling, soaking in;
she presses to me, the winged ants
have moved on to the blackberry bushes clotting the fence,
the cat cleans herself at the end of the bed.

The stone that holds the story of walls in its heart,
the dirt that surrenders air, the water pleas-
ing itself in courtyards and hovels,
that which keeps us alone in grief, alone in the bosom of dark waters,
the sun shining like an axe, day or night,
animals teaching us to be in the world,
viruses teaching us to love--

she presses to me with the fullness of space.

Marc Pietrzykowski lives and works in Niagara County, NY. This is a reissue and reimagining of his first three books of poems.
You can visit Marc virtually at **www.marcpski.com**

Pski's Porch Publishing was formed July 2012, to make books for people who like people who like books. We hope we to have some small successes.

Pski's Porch
323 East Avenue
Lockport, NY 14094
www.pskisporch.com

www.ingramcontent.com/pod-product-compliance
Lightning Source LLC
Chambersburg PA
CBHW060320050426
42449CB00011B/2567